A *WHISTLE* *BLOWER'S* *Requiem*

MICHAEL K. WILLIS

BELLE ISLE BOOKS
www.belleislebooks.com

ISBN: 978-1-953021-57-1
LCCN: 2021923080

Printed in the United States of America

Published by
Belle Isle Books (an imprint of Brandylane Publishers, Inc.)
5 S. 1st Street
Richmond, Virginia 23219

BELLE ISLE BOOKS
www.belleislebook

belleislebooks.com | brandylanepublishers.com

To Tommie Jeanne Davis

PROLOGUE

Wednesday, October 6, 1999, was beautiful. The day was clear, and even though the temperature reached seventy-nine degrees, there was a hint of fall in the air. The humidity was low, and along with a slight breeze, it made for a perfect day. It was a nice break from the sweltering summer days we'd had in Cleveland, Tennessee. Autumn, my favorite time of the year, was on its way. Since childhood, I had always loved it. In my youth, I spent time in the woods near my home to delight in the season, smell the leaves, and enjoy their varied colors. I relished the fresh and chilly air of fall nights. Always a time of joy, autumn contented me, a fondness I carried into my adult years. The weather of that fall day in 1999 still strove to renew my faith and optimism in myself and the world around me, but those positive thoughts were under attack.

The loveliness of the day and the knowledge that autumn lay ahead belied my mood and the anxiety rising within me. I felt weighed down as if I were being pulled into the depths of the sea by an enormous anchor. My chest felt as if a giant were squeezing the life out of me, a creature I could not escape. These and other unsettling thoughts swept through me as I dressed in my business suit and drove from my home in one of the historical neighborhoods near downtown Cleveland and over to Bradley Memorial Hospital, a half-mile north. Was it possible my sixteen-year career there was ending? I had made this short trip every workday since building my home on Seventeenth Street in 1997. My house, set among century-old houses, had the distinction of being new, but you would never know it just by looking. I had built a traditional white Victorian that blended well with the older homes. It was beautiful, the house I had always dreamed of building. I considered it the pinnacle of both my professional and personal success.

During the few minutes it took me to drive to the hospital, I mentally outlined the points of a presentation I hoped to make. I was going to address the Board of Trustees' executive committee.

I had braced myself to shock everyone. Jim Whitlock, the administrator of Bradley Memorial Hospital, my boss, was engaged in illegal activities. He'd made many efforts to enhance hospital revenue through illegal schemes. Federal authorities were looking into the hospital's Medicare reimbursements. State authorities were looking into our TennCare (Tennessee's Medicaid equivalent) billings. Jim was hindering my attempts to change these practices and implement a compliance plan to ensure the hospital found and blocked such illegal schemes.

I had been cooperating with federal and state authorities since July. They were looking at possible illicit hospital practices and alleged criminal activities involving Jim Whitlock. A federal grand jury was hearing evidence in Chattanooga, Tennessee, while the Tennessee District Attorney General was investigating local issues.

These bombshell accusations of compliance fraud were potent not only for their breadth, but also because Bradley Memorial was a public hospital, owned by the citizens of Bradley County. The community had a stake in the outcome. The revelations would set off a public firestorm.

"Compliance" refers to a voluntary program a hospital establishes to protect its operations from fraud and abuse. It encompasses Medicare, Medicaid, and all other federal health programs. The hospital pledges to develop adequate internal controls that promote adherence to federal and state health plans' program requirements and other laws. Its goal is to prevent fraud, abuse, and waste by establishing a culture that promotes prevention, detection, and resolution of instances of conduct that do not conform to these laws.

It was my job to develop a compliance plan for Bradley Memorial Hospital in early 1999. The federal Department of Justice had begun initiatives across the country, targeting hospitals suspected of fraud and abuse. Many high-profile cases had made the news. In neighboring McMinn County, the FBI had raided Woods Memorial Hospital. Bradley Memorial was similarly under investigation for pneumonia billing fraud. Ours was not a raid but an FBI subpoena for records. Senior managers feared, however, that a law enforcement operation could occur at any time. Establishing a voluntary compliance plan would signal to federal authorities that Bradley Memorial was serious about conformity to Medicare regulations.

Even though I was hesitant to take such a project on, Jim Whitlock did not give me a choice about the assignment. From the very beginning, I feared Jim would use these compliance efforts as a ploy to demonstrate conformity while still ignoring the law, and possibly use me as a scapegoat for any violations uncovered by authorities. The hospital's CFO, Craig Taylor, had resigned in February. After Craig left, Jim had blamed him for all the hospital's financial woes and taken no responsibility himself. I worried that this same scenario would play out with me. It became my goal not to let it happen. The best defensive strategy was a good offense, so I set out to enforce compliance. I crafted a comprehensive compliance plan and began aggressively implementing it.

CHAPTER

1

On September 15, before any of the compliance drama had unfolded, Jim Whitlock informed me I was moving out of the executive suite. He was preparing an office for me in a patient room in the oldest wing of the hospital, which was mostly a storage area. Jim did not explain other than to say my executive office would go to someone else. I would have no secretarial support. I suspected the maneuver was just another in a series directed at me in hopes I would leave—but we'll get to that later.

The mostly empty rooms in that wing were dingy and smelled of old urine. Emotionally, I was unprepared for the change. I instructed the maintenance staff not to bother with paint, to just give the room a thorough cleaning. Given my choice of identical, shabby rooms, I selected a room at the end of the wing, close to an exit. Maintenance personnel gave me a key to the adjoining stairwell that allowed me to come and go from the hospital quickly and mostly undetected. As it turned out, my time in this office would be brief.

Moving day was Friday, September 24. I spent most of the day packing and unpacking. Ke Peng, a technician from the Information Technology Department, was already there when I arrived, setting up my computer.

It was clear that what was happening to me distressed Ke. He said, "I don't know if you know this, but I'm a Christian from China. I immigrated here to escape oppression. The authorities persecuted and killed my grandparents during the Cultural Revolution. I really struggled to come to America; I was away from my wife and children for five years. I came here to escape what you are experiencing. To see these things in America is discouraging to me. Be strong. Christians know that God works all things for the good of His children."

I replied, "Thank you for your encouragement, Ke."

Ke's words gave me encouragement, to be sure. But his observation also made me realize that the entire hospital staff was watching these small developments, and the much larger developments that followed.

❖ ❖ ❖

On the afternoon of Monday, September 27. Jim called me into his office for what he described as "a private conversation between the two of us."

"This compliance plan you've written is too hairy! I have to have absolute confidence in our compliance officer. I have no confidence in you at all, and neither do the other senior managers. I've been watching your performance over the past few months, and it's not up to par. Very poor performance! I'm going to look for someone else as compliance officer. Someone I can count on."

I was upset but not surprised. It was a setup but not a betrayal, since the outcome had been clear to me for some time. My mind was in a whirl as I began making my case. I pointed out the many opportunities given him and the other senior managers to supply input into the plan's development. I referenced all the employee code of conduct training sessions I had already led; they were required before any plan could be adopted. I reminded Jim of the hotline I had set up for staff to report suspected fraud and abuse. While I'd done all this work, I had gotten no feedback from them.

As these mandatory code of conduct classes began, I had made a presentation to the senior managers. I'd outlined things that would apply to every employee of the hospital. I specifically mentioned a few examples I knew would get their attention.

"You can't accept free vacations or weekend trips from any company that does business with the hospital. You can't take free Tennessee Volunteer or Tennessee Titans tickets. The value of gifts you receive from vendors has to be nominal; they can't exceed twenty-five dollars."

These restrictions had not gone over well. Every senior manager agreed the limitations needed further discussion before implementation.

"These rules are in both federal and state regulations," I'd argued, "and as a public hospital, we have no recourse but to follow them. These directives will be in my employee code of conduct training sessions."

Jim had left that meeting perturbed. I remembered the whole encounter vividly as I stood before him in his office on that Monday afternoon.

Jim went on to make a telling statement: "You know, we've mainly just tolerated one another for the past eight or nine years because you've always wanted to be administrator. From the moment I was hired!"

I gritted my teeth in frustration before responding. "Well, it's interesting you would say that, and you've told me that before. But it's not true, Jim. Believe it or not. I never applied for the job!"

Jim stared at me with disbelief before pressing on: "Here's what I'm offering. I'll give you six months' severance pay if you leave quietly.

Like, by Friday, October 1. I need your decision by 5 p.m. tomorrow. Realistically, Michael, this is an offer you need to consider seriously. I don't see a place for you at the hospital in the future. I'm going to cut out your assistant administrator position. There's going to be another wave of layoffs, and as I see it, you're low on the totem pole. I have to have people working for me who are *loyal*."

I was shaken by his statement. "Jim, you know I've always been loyal to Bradley Memorial Hospital."

"That's not what I'm talking about!" Jim appeared to be demanding personal loyalty, something he and I would never give one another—not after all the trouble we'd given each other.

To avoid making a rash commitment, I said, "It's impossible to make this kind of decision in twenty-four hours. There's too much to think about. I'll have to talk to my wife."

"Well, you have until 5 p.m. tomorrow," Jim replied.

I couldn't believe what I was hearing, even from Jim. The words burst out of me before I could consider them. "Well! If that's all the time you're giving me, then I'll give you my answer now. No!"

I could tell from Jim's startled look that my quick decision took him by surprise, and his mouth flapped momentarily as he struggled to choose what to say next.

"Ah!" said Jim at last, clearly having reassessed his obstinance. "Okay! Well, I'm willing to add a few caveats and give you until the end of the week. But you can't use the time to make this political. Don't call Gary Davis or Bill Ledford. You can't contact the members of the Board of Trustees. If you do any of that, I'll fire you on the spot!"

"Jim, I simply can't accept those terms. Six months is too short to realistically find another job. Besides that, I want to talk to some of my allies to know if they support you or not. My answer is still no."

"Ugh," Jim sneered. "You're taking a big risk. Listen, Michael: there isn't room in this hospital for both of us. Either you'll be gone, or

I'll be gone, and if you can pull it off, so be it."

Jim was challenging me. I interpreted his statement to mean that if I had the political influence to oust him from his job, I was welcome to try. I thought, *Jim, I don't know if I can get you fired or not, but I'll do my best.*

Jim went on: "I don't know what the next three months will bring. They could fire me; they could fire you. You could end up administrator, or someone else could end up administrator. Everything right now is that uncertain!" After Jim saw I was not going to budge, he concluded in exasperation, "You know, I'm not surprised you said no. I expected you would."

"Then why did you ask? Is there anything else, Jim?"

Jim lowered his head in frustration and disappointment and said, "No."

I waited for Jim to say something else, but when he didn't raise his head, I knew our encounter was over. I walked out of Jim's office.

❖ ❖ ❖

I at once began developing a strategy to deal with this extraordinary situation. The plan was simple. Make personal calls or visits to all members of the Board of Trustees, the hospital attorney, and the county executive. I believed a straightforward approach, including documented evidence, would go a long way in giving my case credibility.

County Executive Gary Davis was already aware of federal and state investigations involving the hospital when I met with him in his office later that day. He advocated for an immediate political response to Jim's ultimatum. "The feds are looking into the hospital's pneumonia billing practices and other possible criminal issues. The DA's office is doing a parallel criminal investigation. They'll wait for the federal grand jury to act first. It meets the first of every month down in Chattanooga. The FBI might conduct a raid over at the hospital in a month or so. That means nothing is likely to happen before then."

"Gary," I said, trying to keep the exasperation from my voice, "that timeline doesn't work well with my situation. Jim wants to settle this by next week! I'll meet with the board members, encourage them to study the issues I raise, and give them a chance to act. If that fails, then we can move to political pressure."

Gary agreed to allow my approach first, although he was skeptical of it, preferring an immediate political attack. "Sam Bettis is very close to Jim Whitlock," Gary warned.

Sam had been the hospital's board chairman for many years. He enjoyed the status of the position enormously. Sam was a mechanical engineer who worked at Bowater, Inc., a paper mill in Calhoun, Tennessee. Sam was arrogant, condescending, and sarcastic. He always thought he was the smartest person in the room. Despite these tendencies, Jim Whitlock had forged a close relationship with him, as had previous Bradley Memorial administrators. It seemed each were able to brush Sam's ego just enough to get his support on most issues.

I agreed with Gary's assessment of Sam, but I replied, "I still believe some of the board members are open to persuasion."

"I wouldn't count on Lou Patten to support you either," Gary replied. He gathered that my next argument would be to point out my friendship with Lou.

Lou Patten was a local insurance broker and principal partner in his own company. As the agent for Bradley Memorial's property and casualty insurance, he had a serious conflict of interest when he began serving as a board member, an issue that was kept quiet from other board members and the public. Lou was also politically well-connected as a former Republican state senator. I considered Lou not only a friend but also a political ally. We had worked well together during the years I'd run the local Republican Party and he served as state senator.

"You may be right about Lou, Gary." I remembered Lou sometimes surprised me by supporting or opposing legislation on which I thought we agreed. "But I believe it's important to talk to the board first."

❖ ❖ ❖

Over the next few days, I met with six of the seven board members. Only Sam Bettis refused to meet, which was a disturbing development, but given what Gary had said, it was not surprising. All but one board member expressed alarm and concern.

The first board member I spoke with was Eddie Duncan, M.D. He was cautious about speaking with me but revealed, "I'm surprised Jim has never brought any of these issues to the board. These are serious matters."

Eddie was an ophthalmologist who represented the medical staff on the Board of Trustees. Before his appointment to the board, Eddie had served in many leadership roles among the hospital physicians, including chief of staff.

Next I spoke with Don Lorton, chairman of the board's finance committee. "Talk to Lou Patten as soon as you can," he advised. "We're close, he and I. Don't rest until you've spoken with every board member."

Before his retirement, Don Lorton had been president of the local Maytag plant (later Whirlpool), a global manufacturer of appliances. Don brought his years of manufacturing experience to the Board of Trustees, which was a rare asset.

The next board member on my list was Bob Cantrell, who was a colleague of Sam's and the safety director at Bowater, Inc. He said diplomatically, "There's a real need for leadership change at the hospital."

Heeding Don Lorton's advice, I talked at length with Lou Patten. Don had already briefed him by the time we spoke, but there was still much to examine. We discussed a letter he had circulated in June that had called for Jim Whitlock's resignation. Lou agreed to distribute it among the Board of Trustees once more to gauge their support.

"I'm going to discuss strategy with Don before I do anything," Lou said.

I was pleased that Don and Lou both seemed to be on my side, but I was still nervous. "Lou, if there are any meetings set to discuss these issues, please make sure I'm there."

Lou agreed.

After my conversation with Lou, I had renewed hope for my conversation with Bob Sain. In that meeting Bob said bluntly, "It's apparent: Jim needs to go."

Bob Sain had retired from retail management, as he'd been the store manager at J.C. Penney's. A pleasant man, Bob often asked smart and probing questions when it came to board matters. Optimistic by nature, he usually looked for the good in everyone. Bob liked Jim Whitlock, and they worked well together—but you could say the same of Bob and anyone. Because of Bob's relationship with Jim, his negative comment both took me by surprise and encouraged me.

Of all the board members, only Bobbie Atchley, the newest, was noncommittal when I explained my position to her. But she listened attentively. The county commission had recently selected Bobbie to replace Gary Davis, who had resigned from the hospital board following his election as county executive. Bobbie, a retiree, had served as a nurse manager at the hospital before her appointment. Most senior managers had been against her selection because she had worked at a management level beneath them. Jim also expressed his anxiety about the choice. Still, I suspected he was posturing; Bobbie, as an employee, was one of his biggest supporters.

"Bobbie," I said when it became clear I couldn't sway her, "I'd encourage you to discuss these matters with the other board members and make a fair judgment."

Finally, on the morning of Wednesday, September 29, I talked with Mike Callaway. Because he was the hospital's attorney, I crafted a different approach. I was there to inform Mike of severe compliance issues about Administrator Jim Whitlock and Bradley Memorial Hospital.

Many of the issues I raised were already under review by the investigators, while others were new. However, all involved Jim. (I would find out later that Mike Callaway was already aware of the state criminal investigation and an FBI probe when I spoke to him that day.)

"Mike," I said frankly, "Jim is attempting to get me to resign. He's threatened to fire me if I don't. Firing the compliance officer would be bad for the hospital."

"I'll call Sam Bettis and Don Lorton and inform them we have a problem," Mike replied.

I concluded these meetings hopeful they'd had an impact. It did not take long to find out.

❖ ❖ ❖

After meeting with Mike Callaway, I was in and out of the hospital as I continued with various meetings, most of which concerned the current crisis. In the afternoon, I returned to discover the lock on my office door had been changed. I could not get in. I made my way to Jim's office and found him in a hostile mood.

"You threatened a lawsuit!" were Jim's first words.

"No," I replied levelly, choosing my words carefully, "that's not true. I'm the hospital's compliance officer. I informed Mike of serious violations here at Bradley Memorial. Now, firing me could have legal ramifications. I told him that, but I wasn't threatening a lawsuit. He'll have to clear it up."

"You're not the compliance officer!" Jim replied angrily.

"Jim, you appointed me! You told me to construct and implement a plan, which I've done. Now, it's true: the plan calls for a board-appointed compliance officer once it's adopted. Still—right now, I am the hospital's compliance officer. No one else is! Why else would I have done all this work? Why else would I have been training employees?"

Jim retorted, "The compliance plan is not ready for the Board of Trustees' approval."

"But I've given you and the entire senior management team many opportunities to review it, offer input, make changes. I've heard nothing from any of you. To meet the deadline that *you* set, I've already mailed copies to the board for their review and approval."

"Listen, Michael," Jim snarled, "the compliance plan will be what *I* decide it will be, and I'm telling you it's not ready. Sam told me he hasn't even read it. It will not be on the board's agenda! Until we can get things sorted out, get the board to look at all this, I am putting you on paid leave. Once I set the meeting, I'll expect you to be there. I'll be bringing up your threat to sue the hospital. And we'll be discussing your poor job performance. Don't come back to the hospital until the meeting. Do *not* discuss this with anybody. I know you've discussed our Monday meeting, and it has gotten all over the hospital. And I know who you've been talking to."

Indeed, I had talked to several different managers and employees at the hospital. It was a strategic decision. I only shared the information I wanted to distribute. I knew one or more of them would take what I'd said back to Jim, which they clearly had. I was okay with that too.

"Make sure Mike Callaway is at the meeting," I told him.

"I'll let you know when I schedule it," Jim replied.

❖ ❖ ❖

In the days after I went on administrative leave, there were strategy sessions and phone calls among some of the board members. Lou Paten told me about these meetings.

Bob Sain, Don Lorton, and Lou met to discuss Jim's future status. All agreed that Jim Whitlock could not continue as the hospital administrator. They also decided to seek a meeting with Sam Bettis to express their concerns.

Lou said, "Michael, when we met with Sam, he pushed back hard. He told us, 'I didn't call Michael Willis back when he called. He threatened a lawsuit when he talked to Mike Callaway.'"

Lou continued, "Sam also said, 'I've heard no concerns from any other hospital manager regarding Jim's leadership, and I won't support any effort to remove him.'"

It was clear. Sam Bettis's support for Jim Whitlock was reliable.

Regarding Sam's position, Lou Patton said, "Michael, we won't take any action against Jim Whitlock as long as Sam Bettis supports him."

Lou's comment was alarming and disappointing. It was news I had not expected, but I still was not ready to give up.

Jim Whitlock and other senior managers set out to keep the matter quiet. They warned all department heads and nurse managers not to discuss any rumors they were hearing. I only learned of this because not all of the department heads complied. One department director said to me, "The senior managers are using Gestapo tactics to keep this silent."

Their plan did not work. Hospital employees and physicians began making calls in earnest to the Board of Trustees, County Executive Gary Davis, and county commission members. Many people reached out to me too, both those making these calls and those receiving them. They were encouraging across the board.

In a follow-up discussion with Gary Davis, he told me it was time to get the county commission to act. He would encourage them to make calls to board members too.

As a county facility, Bradley Memorial Hospital fell under the ownership of the Bradley County Commission, an elected body. Its members' opinions were always considerable when it came to hospital issues. The brewing issue had raised much concern.

On Wednesday afternoon, October 6, I finally received a call at home from Juanita Burris, Jim's administrative assistant. She told me to be at CFO Ken Jackson's office at 5:30 p.m.; the Board of Trustees' executive committee would be meeting then.

"Will I have an opportunity to speak to the board members at this meeting?" I asked.

"I'll have to find out."

Juanita placed my call on hold. After a few minutes, she returned and said, "Jim says the board is meeting at 5 p.m. You can come early in the event they want to hear from you."

It was not a good sign. Jim had changed the rules. Earlier, he'd said I should be ready to address the group. Now Jim was hedging, wanting me there after the meeting was underway.

Later that day, Don Lorton told one of my friends that all the train cars were not in a row on this issue. He was referring to Sam Bettis's continued support of Jim and opposition to my challenge.

It was clear the meeting was being rushed.

I made a call to County Executive Gary Davis. He was not aware of the meeting but said he would "crash the party."

"It's clear Jim's strategy is to make the issue about me," I responded, "but if I get the opportunity, I'll make it all about compliance and legal matters."

I arrived at Ken Jackson's office, where he and I waited for more than an hour while the Board of Trustees' executive committee met.

All the board members but one attended, although it was technically an executive committee meeting, and not all of them were required to attend. Bobbie Atchley was the only person absent. Everyone except me was surprised when Gary Davis showed up.

Because Bradley Memorial was a public hospital, the law required the board to publish all their meetings' dates and times, including committee meetings, before they occurred, allowing the public and press the opportunity to attend. Routinely, however, the hospital only announced the formal, monthly Board of Trustees meetings, and never executive committee meetings. The local media had never challenged this practice. For this reason, I assumed the meeting was set up as an executive committee meeting to avoid making a public announcement.

Jim Whitlock, Mike Callaway, and consultant Steve Spargo with Compliance Concepts, Inc. also attended. Bradley Memorial had been using Steve's consulting group for the past two years to help assess the hospital's Medicare vulnerabilities. Jim wanted Steve to review the compliance plan I had prepared for approval on behalf of the board.

While we waited, I asked Ken Jackson what he thought the outcome of the executive committee meeting would be.

Ken didn't look pleased when he told me. "Jim intends to make the case that your compliance efforts have been poor, and since you threatened to file a lawsuit against the hospital, he's recommending termination. Once the meeting ends, he plans to come in here and fire you. Jim has been trying to get rid of you since the layoff in June. He and the others have been making the case against you since then."

I was upset but not surprised to hear the news. All my suspicions about Jim's motives for placing me in charge of compliance were about to come true. My mind raced back through the sixteen years I had been at the hospital and wondered how it could be ending like this.

Ken was upset too. He fidgeted and had a tough time making eye contact. I asked what was troubling him.

Looking across my shoulder and at the wall behind me, Ken confided, "I wouldn't have come to Bradley Memorial if I'd known what I know now. Jim and the entire senior management team have no credibility with the community, the medical staff, or the employees. We have a divided board. I don't believe Jim will survive to the end of the year." Appearing even more distressed and finally looking directly at me, Ken continued, "Michael, of everyone that Jim and the others are worried about, you give them the most anxiety, unease, and fear. You stand alone in the hospital as the most critical person to watch, the one person who causes the most grief. Jim and the others have been nervous about the idea of you being the compliance officer. I know they don't want that."

An odd sense of pride swept over me on hearing of their trepidation. *At least they fear me for my integrity, for always doing what I believe is right*, I thought.

Ken continued, "While the board has rebuffed Jim many times, he's still intent on selling or leasing Bradley Memorial. He wants to sell to either CHS or Memorial Hospital in Chattanooga." CHS stood for Community Health Systems, a for-profit hospital chain based in Nashville, Tennessee. "Jim has met several times with the CEO at Cleveland Community Hospital. Since CHS owns that hospital, it would be the most interested party. They would like to pull off an arrangement that would avoid a public bid. I don't think the board has the stomach to do the things necessary to save the hospital. I believe these proposals will soon get sincere consideration."

I sensed, as Ken continued talking, that he was feeling somewhat better by getting these matters off his chest. Perhaps, finally, he had found someone who understood his own misgivings about Jim and his team.

I was soon called into the executive committee meeting. Later, Gary Davis would tell me that in the gathering, prior to my arrival, consultant Steve Spargo spent more than an hour highlighting what he viewed as deficiencies in the compliance document I had crafted. He assured the board that all the issues I had raised in our private meetings were not serious. Jim Whitlock then called on Mike Callaway, who told the group he felt I had threatened a lawsuit against Bradley Memorial Hospital. From Gary's point of view, Jim's surrogates were making a compelling case against me. Gary said, "The meeting was about to adjourn when Lou Patten said, 'I don't feel right adjourning this meeting before we hear from Michael.'"

A tense moment followed before they agreed I could come into the meeting.

I entered a somber assemblage. The board's conference room was a place in which I had made many presentations. This talk, however, rang with a sense of finality. If I wasn't successful, my career at Bradley Memorial was over.

I looked down the long conference table. Gary Davis nodded, and Lou Patten smiled. I returned their acknowledgements. Sam and Jim looked nervous but determined. They shifted their eyes back and forth at each other. Steve Spargo looked at me with amusement. Most of the others kept their heads down.

Sam began by simply asking me if I had anything to say. He said nothing more. Even though I could feel the tensity, I wasn't nervous but rather filled with a sense of resolve.

I began my defense, not knowing what had just been discussed.

"Jim Whitlock is engaged in illegal activities," I started strongly. "His efforts to enhance hospital revenue through various schemes are many. Federal authorities are looking into the hospital's Medicare reimbursements. State authorities are looking into our TennCare billings. Jim has been blocking my attempts to change hospital practices and implement a compliance plan to ensure that we identify and stop such illegal schemes. Jim has alleged I threatened a lawsuit, but when I met with Mike Callaway, I did no such thing. I did point out the obvious: terminating the compliance officer could have serious legal ramifications for the hospital."

Mike Callaway offered no counterargument to my statement, but Steve Spargo responded: "It's my expert opinion that none of the issues you've raised are serious. The Medicare and TennCare problems you highlighted are routine, nothing more. You took a template given you by Compliance Concepts and turned it into your own, a simple cookie cutter approach with no real insight as how it affects this particular hospital."

"Mr. Spargo," I countered, turning to him, "it's clear to me why you would make that argument. After all, Jim Whitlock is paying you to say it."

Before I could announce my cooperation with federal and state investigators, Gary Davis spoke up. "Many things are being investigated by both federal and local authorities. I've met with them on many occasions. This investigation is real, and it is serious. Investigators are certain there will be charges. Interviews have been held with others in this room too."

Gary's statements were explosive. Sam Bettis and Jim Whitlock became ashen gray. Steve Spargo looked as if his eyes would bug out of his head. Clearly, this was news to a lot of people but not all.

"Well, I have to admit, the FBI interviewed me," Bob Sain confessed.

"I met with them too," Eddie Duncan said.

Stunned and shaken by these revelations, Sam adjourned the meeting at once. Everyone left in a hurry. I went home. It was not clear what would happen next.

❖ ❖ ❖

Nothing happened the next day, but on Friday, October 8, I got a call from Juanita Burris.

"Mr. Whitlock wants to meet with you today at 3:30 p.m."

She did not say what the meeting would cover.

I called Lou Patten. I knew he would know what was going on.

"The board met again and decided it would only deal with Jim Whitlock about this issue. All other personnel matters will be left up to him," Lou stated.

Although Lou had helped me at the board's executive committee meeting, Gary had been right about him. I should never have thought I could trust him. Gary had seen this side of him before, and I had seen hints of it.

"What is the 3:30 p.m. meeting about?" I asked.

"The meeting is to give you a severance package and terminate your employment," Lou responded coldly.

"Lou, how can you let this happen? You know what Jim is doing is illegal. What is going on here?"

"I've done all I can," Lou replied. "I want Jim out, but none of the other board members will go along. So, this is their decision!"

To say I was disappointed with Lou is an understatement. I knew he could have done more. I felt betrayed by Lou's callous response.

I called Mike Callaway from home. I was still on paid administrative leave. I asked him about the upcoming meeting with Jim.

"It's an exit interview. You will have to disclose all legal issues you've been involved in personally. If you don't, by law, you cannot file a lawsuit."

"Okay, Mike," I said slowly, thinking through my options. "I can disclose enough to get your attention. It would have come out at the executive committee meeting if it had not adjourned so abruptly. I've been cooperating with the District Attorney General's office since July, and I've met with the FBI and the Tennessee Bureau of Investigation."

Mike was silent for a moment and then said, "Ah. I'm on my way to the hospital right now to talk to Jim. Can I call you back?"

"Sure."

About thirty minutes later, Mike called me.

"Your meeting with Jim is off. I'll call you again in a little while."

Instead of calling a third time, Mike came to my home near downtown Cleveland. Mike had never come to my house before, but his office was just a few blocks away, and apparently he felt the urgency to come by.

I noticed Mike pull into my driveway, went to a side door that led into the kitchen, and motioned for him to come in. He was agitated and excited as he entered the kitchen, appearing out of breath.

After asking a perfunctory question as to how I was doing and not waiting for an answer, Mike said as we stood there, "I spoke with the DA's office to confirm your story. I went to the hospital to tell Jim not to take action against you. Now I'm on my way to inform each board member this issue is before them, and they will have to deal with it. I told Jim to put you back to work, but he would not have it. He said it would be too divisive. Instead, you will stay on paid administrative leave until the board deals with the matter of Jim Whitlock. I also instructed Jim not to remove any hospital documents. I've got to go meet with board members now. I'll be your hospital contact as we move forward."

Mike was in a hurry to leave as I said, "Thanks for letting me know. I hope to hear from you soon." I didn't.

And that is where my status remained for the next three months.

CHAPTER
2

How I arrived at this place in my career requires an explanation, the complications of which are difficult to disentangle. It was like a sudden volcano. The signs of an explosion had been there for years; yet, when it happened, everyone was shocked as tiny bits of wreckage came falling from the sky.

Or better yet, it was an anthill. On the outside, the situation seemed tranquil enough, but once the hill was kicked over, ants came pouring out in all directions.

It might have been easier to accept the severance pay and move on, but for me, it was not an option. Quitting was not in my DNA. I grew up in a physically and emotionally abusive family that turned me into a fighter. I fought—at home, at school, in the streets. It was always my first response to danger. I didn't like to fight but did so as a means to protect myself. I was not a bully, but no one could bully me either. Once I was locked into a fight, it was a total commitment—no backing down, a fight to the finish. This attitude dominated my adolescent years, and I carried it into my working career, particularly if I perceived an injustice. At the beginning of my career, at a critical juncture, just once, I went against this instinct. I always regretted my decision. It would never happen again.

Jim Whitlock may not have known I was a warrior, but he probably did. We had worked together for many years. Jim likely knew my nature and chose to challenge me anyway. He felt he had no other choice. The circumstances Jim faced were extreme. They required bold, risky moves. Jim hoped I would give in but feared I would not.

❖ ❖ ❖

I came to Cleveland and Bradley County in the spring of 1971, when I helped my family move there from Franklin, North Carolina. My father, Reverend John R. Willis, Jr., a Baptist preacher, had gone to Cleveland to escape a scandal of his own making that involved another woman. He had abandoned my mother and siblings that previous January. Six of eight children were still living at home, including me. I had just completed my first year of college at Western Carolina University in Cullowhee, North Carolina. I commuted from home. My father's illicit relationship soon failed, and he moved to Tennessee to reestablish himself, hoping the news from Franklin would not follow him. He obtained the help of an old childhood friend, a fellow Baptist preacher, who had pastored in the area for years. Soon my dad was back in business, pastoring Tasso Baptist Church. No one in Cleveland ever found out about Dad's past.

At the same time, my father reached out to my mother, implored her to come back to him and move to Cleveland. Heartbroken, but with nowhere else to go, Mother consented. She still had young children to raise.

Out of college for the summer, I helped with the packing and moving. My brother-in-law and I took turns driving a rented moving truck to Cleveland, a three-hour drive. We arrived to a great disturbance. Police officers were everywhere. We came into town from the east, along Highway 64, right through Sixth Ward, an African American community, where the conflict was taking place. The police stopped us, and we were told to turn around, to leave Cleveland. I was driving.

"We can't turn around," I explained. "We're moving here."

"What part of town are you moving to?" the officer asked.

"Across town, to Willow Street," I replied.

Eventually, the officers allowed us to pass. "Be careful as you drive through Sixth Ward," they warned.

"Is this a riot? What kind of place are we moving to?" I asked my brother-in-law rhetorically. Only later did I learn what I had seen was an anomaly. Race relations in Cleveland were generally good.

When we got to the tiny rental house, Mother exclaimed, "God built Cleveland, Tennessee, over hell." She was referring to the heat, which was oppressive to us. Cleveland was hotter and much more humid than the Blue Ridge Mountains.

The next day, after helping unpack, I headed back to Franklin, North Carolina. I stayed with my sister and brother-in-law. I worked a summer job before returning to my sophomore year at Western Carolina University.

Getting a college education was especially important to me. I saw it as a way out of my very harsh upbringing. Schooling was the only thing that could rescue me. I was able to go to college only because of the Pell Grant program, which provided funds for students with exceptional financial need. I also got money from the National Defense Student Loan Program (later renamed the National Direct Student Loan Program), which offered low-interest loans to those same students. I saw college as my path to a better life, and I was willing to work anywhere during the summer months to earn my degree.

In college, I pursued politics, government, and history, subjects that had always interested me in high school. In the summers, I worked at Magic Chef, an appliance manufacturer (later Maytag and now Whirlpool), in the steel room that fabricated parts. This job allowed me to get to know Cleveland, and it was instrumental in my eventual permanent relocation to the city. I graduated from Western Carolina University in 1974 with a double major bachelor's in political science and history, and in 1976 from the University of Tennessee with a master's degree in public administration. After finishing my graduate degree, I came to Cleveland to look for a job.

My first inclination was to return to my native western North Carolina, to Asheville, and look for work there. I might have done that, but for the love of a woman.

In the summer of 1974, I met a woman from Cleveland. She was a teacher with the Bradley County School System and working on a master's degree in education at the University of Tennessee. Her charm, beauty, intelligence, and good nature attracted me. In 1975, this love interest was in Knoxville finishing her final semester while I was just beginning. After completing my degree in 1976, Cleveland became my only choice for finding employment because of this woman. I got a job working for the Bradley County Judge. As it turned out, my relationship with the teacher ended, but not before I had become firmly planted in Cleveland. For the next two decades I remained a bachelor, not marrying until 1994.

When I first started working, I found my new boss, County Judge Carl Colloms, to be an odd person. Bald, small, and beady-eyed, with a quirky personality, he was hard to envision as a successful politician. I was surprised the voters had elected him. He ran for office using one chief credential—he was the county attorney. Carl had argued that a professional should occupy the position even though the office was mostly administrative. The confusion with the title was enough to help him win.

I became the director of a jobs program. The work entailed hiring and training summer youth, young adults, and adults who had been out of the workforce for many years. Terry Gallaher directed a similar program that concentrated on recently unemployed adults. Funding for these programs came from the Comprehensive Employment and Training Act (CETA), a federal jobs program that dispensed grants to the states. CETA became law in response to a recession that had plagued the economy during the latter part of the 1970s. Tennessee received its share of these federal dollars and then dispensed money to counties to run local programs. Since manufacturing was the primary source for employment, the community was particularly susceptible to recession. The temporary CETA jobs of the 1970s were popular and helped relieve the strain of that downturn.

I was fortunate to get the job. I believed working there would be an enjoyable experience, the beginning of a successful career in government. I did not count on the education it would give me in local governmental workings, or at least this particular local county government.

Terry Gallaher's program quickly became political. The only criteria for getting a job were six months of unemployment and certification by the Department of Employment Security. Those who knew the county judge, a county commissioner, or any other elected official got first consideration. It became a source of patronage.

My program could not be political due to the more rigorous participation requirements, including a low-income standard each participant had to meet. There were times I could not fill all the job openings. These constraints shielded my program, and I was glad for it. I did not like the politics of Terry's job.

I was familiar with government structure and government on the federal, state, and local levels from my political science and public administration studies. It was a theoretical knowledge, as I had never worked for a governmental entity before. During the years I worked for Bradley County, I got on-the-job working experience. It was far different from my academic view, but the government still fascinated me.

I reasoned I should continue working in government because ethical people were vitally needed in public service.

Attending county commission meetings made me aware of the growing need for new schools, roads, recreational parks, industrial parks, jails, and other infrastructure. It was clear; tremendous growth was erupting. Having studied these issues in college, I was naturally curious to see how a government would solve them. I was surprised at the process, although in retrospect, I should not have been.

The politics of a privileged few dominated every facet of government. Each infrastructure improvement decision was made based on which individuals would personally profit.

The county budget was also political and was used to reward supporters. Nonexistent positions appeared with full pay and benefits. One individual in such a position supplied security for one of the county's softball parks. He came by the courthouse twice a month to pick up his checks but did not show up at the park very often.

None of these issues directly affected me. I was only an observer. I concentrated on my CETA program. I was determined to run it with the highest ethical standards, and things went well for a time.

Terry Gallaher approached me about a savings plan his brother offered to all county employees, including his CETA employees. It was easy; deductions would come right out of an employee's paycheck.

"My brother wants a list of your employees to offer it to them too," he said.

"Give me a copy of the plan. I'll review it first," I replied.

In evaluating the proposal, it was clear to me CETA employees would get no benefit from it. The plan was an annuity, which required monthly employee contributions for five years. Early termination meant giving up all employee premiums. CETA jobs were temporary, lasting no more than a year. Few of these employees went onto the regular county payroll after they completed the program. For them to sign up for the annuity meant an almost certain loss of their entire investment.

I finally said, "No, Terry, your brother can't have access to my employees. The plan is not right for them."

My decision did not go over well. Terry's face reddened with anger as he pursed his lips and said, "We'll see about that." He stomped out of my office.

Terry later returned to my office and said, "The judge said for you to turn over your employee list."

"If Judge Colloms wants it," I responded firmly, "then he'll have to ask for it himself. Until then, you will not get it."

I never heard from Carl Colloms. After that, my relationships with Carl and Terry, which had always been tricky, became severely strained. Over the next several weeks, pressure mounted from them and others. I was no longer invited to lunch, which had been routine. Office doors, which had always been open to me, were shut. I could not get appointments to discuss CETA program issues. Terry gathered with office staff behind closed doors. Coworkers were assigned to document my comings and goings. When I asked the secretary why she was watching me, she sneered, lifted their shoulders, and said, "Judge's orders!" with a great jeering smile on her face. The situation became untenable.

To gauge my legal standing, I had state CETA program officials evaluate the annuity plan. They agreed my response was appropriate but refused to intervene, seeing it as a local issue. With their decision not to support me, I had few options.

As it had been in my youth, my instinct was to fight, not to give in, but this was different. I saw three options. I could take the issue to the county commission while exposing it to the press, I could stay on and try to weather the storm, or I could resign and move on. Going to the county commission and making it a media event seemed sensible except that Carl Colloms' standing in the community was remarkably high. I knew he could get the issue dismissed as that of a disgruntled employee. I had seen other cases handled this way. Without state CETA officials backing me up, I decided not to go this route.

Staying on quickly became senseless. The harassment was too much. Bewildered by what was happening, I decided to resign. It was a decision I regretted from the moment I made it. I soon wished I had stayed and figured out another solution. But it was too late. I had already turned in my notice, and I knew Carl Colloms would not let me rescind it. To my great regret, I also realized that my resignation had left my workers exposed. These vulnerable employees would soon hear about the plan. Not knowing what the future held, I vowed never to allow such a thing to happen again. The next time, I would fight.

After a period, I landed back on my feet with a new job at Bradley Memorial Hospital. Looking back, I realized this hospital job might not have come my way if I had gotten into a nasty public fight with the county judge. I began working in this position on January 18, 1984.

CHAPTER
3

B radley County Memorial Hospital was a private act hospital created in 1947 by the Tennessee General Assembly. Such an act was passed by the state legislative body but applied to a single county. The law allowed hospital bonds to be issued to construct a facility once a majority of voters approved. After the referendum passed, a Board of Trustees oversaw the development and later the hospital's operations. The authorities added several amendments to the private act that expanded the board and specified the appointment method. By 1999, there were seven board members: four appointed by the Bradley County Commission, two by the Cleveland City Council, and one by the hospital medical staff. It was traditional for one county commissioner to serve on such a board. At the time of my employment, County Commissioner Bill Ledford served in this role and was an essential friend and ally of the hospital administrator, Bill Torrence.

Bill Ledford was supposed to be the county commission's eyes and ears on the Board of Trustees. Instead, he was the most significant figure advocating for the hospital's interests. Disabled by an automobile accident early in life, Bill used his time cutting deals among county commissioners. He successfully pushed every measure involving Bradley Memorial through the county commission. Bill was a key partner for Bill Torrence and eventually Howard Kuhns, who followed Bill Torrence as the administrator. After Jim Whitlock was elevated to the role, he too took extraordinary steps to befriend Bill. Jim was mostly successful, although Bill was wary of his interest in selling the hospital.

When building the new hospital, trustees took advantage of funds made available by a federal law known as the Hill-Burton Act. In exchange for these grants and loans, Bradley Memorial had to supply a reasonable volume of services to people who could not pay. They also had to make their services available to all residents of its service area. It was a law that brought healthcare services to much of rural America for the first time.

The fifty-two-bed hospital opened for business in December 1952. Bill Torrence, who had been the purchasing agent for Erlanger Hospital in Chattanooga, soon became the administrator. He had been there for more than thirty years by the time I arrived.

From the time the hospital opened, there was conflict between the hospital and Bradley County. Differences, articulated primarily by County Judge Mark Fulbright, centered around finances and control. Primarily an administrative job, the office of the county judge was eventually changed by the Tennessee General Assembly to county executive. Judge Fulbright often clashed with Bill Torrence, arguing that excess funds from operations had to go to the elected county trustee each year for investment. The county commission would determine the use of that money. On the other hand, Bill Torrence understood the importance of cash reserves to the hospital's operations. He secured the approval of the entire Board of Trustees in resisting all efforts to transfer funds.

The dispute arose from a section of the private act. It directed the hospital trustees to hand over any profits or funds to the county trustee after keeping such amount as necessary or advisable for working capital. There lay the issue. The county judge and many county commissioners believed the amount set aside should be minimal. On the other hand, Bill Torrence always budgeted, with board approval, an amount that set the cash reserves requirement higher than they could reach. This strategy always denied the county any excess profits. Over the years, this policy continued to be a source of contention, but no one ever took legal action on the issue.

The dispute over who controlled excess profits also drove the hospital's financial strategy, causing Bill Torrence to take a conservative approach toward the charges of hospital patients. He did not want extra profits to be so high as to trigger a legal challenge from the county. Over time, Bradley Memorial became the lowest-cost healthcare provider in the entire region to avoid this likelihood. The strategy also contributed to the hospital's future financial problems.

There was also an issue over the hospital's purchasing procedures. Bradley County was under the Purchasing Act of 1952. The county judge was to appoint a purchasing agent, usually himself, to oversee all purchasing. Judge Fulbright declared that the hospital, as a county institution, must abide by this act, subjecting it to his considerable influence. Bill Torrence and the hospital trustees pushed back, asserting that the private act that created the hospital stipulated an independent body, as demonstrated by a separate board. They were then responsible for setting up their procedures. This issue, also never litigated, continued to be a point of dispute throughout the years.

Downplaying the hospital's legal ties to Bradley County became a key strategy. The decision had far-reaching implications for the hospital's future. The hospital's marketing approach was to disassociate itself from the county. The private act established the name of the institution as Bradley *County* Memorial Hospital. However, Bill Torrence dropped the word "County" from its signage and advertising. The hospital became Bradley Memorial Hospital. Only legal documents used the full title.

One area in which the hospital could not escape its ties to Bradley County was in the issuance of hospital bonds. Building projects, by legal necessity, continued to come to the county legislative body. After several expansions, the county commission became increasingly resistant to issuing these bonds since Bradley County was solely responsible for their repayment. To ease their concern, Bradley Memorial instead began requesting authorization to issue hospital *revenue* bonds. These revenue bonds placed the financial burden directly on the hospital since future hospital revenue would repay them. Through the years, Bradley Memorial grew to two hundred and fifty-one beds using hospital revenue bonds. This strategy was an acceptable alternative for both the Board of Trustees and the county commissioners. The arrangement meant the county was only a secondary payer, in case of a total hospital collapse, and gave the hospital the freedom needed to continue growing. But, over time, it too set a precedent that contributed to the hospital's final financial woes.

❖ ❖ ❖

I initially began working as the hospital's director of human resources. My experience running the CETA program for the county was instrumental in my selection. I was happy to get the job. I planned to settle into the role, learn about the hospital operations, and, hopefully, move up into administration over time. I was surprised when after only three months, Bill Torrence called me to his office. Associate Administrator Howard Kuhns was there too.

Bill asked, "You know our assistant administrator has submitted his resignation, don't you?" This assistant administrator had hired me.

"Yes, I understand he's the new administrator of a hospital in Virginia."

"That's right. He will be leaving in a month," Bill replied. "My question, Michael, is why haven't you applied for the assistant administrator position? We think you'd make a great candidate for the job."

"Yes, we do," Howard interjected.

"Wow! I'm honored. Thank you for having faith in me. When I heard about the assistant administrator leaving, I was interested, but I didn't think you'd consider me. I've only been here three months!"

"I understand that, but Howard and I want you to apply anyway. Bring me a copy of your resume."

That conversation was the beginning of an interview process with board members to gain their support.

Bill Torrence sent me to interview with three of the seven board members, including Herbert Lackey, a teacher at Bradley Central High School. All the meetings were pleasant. I wondered why Bill wanted me to see these three.

Afterward, I asked him, "Is there anyone else I need to see?"

"No," Bill replied confidently. "The other board members will support my decision. Bill Ledford speaks very highly of you from your time working for Judge Colloms and attending county commission meetings. It was important to shore up the support of these three. Sometimes it's a little tricky dealing with them."

Bill Torrence announced my hiring at the next board meeting.

❖ ❖ ❖

I did not know at that time that Herbert Lackey was also lobbying to get the job. Bill Torrence later told me that the other two trustees were open to hiring him. My interviews aimed to shut down Herbert's efforts without my knowledge. Bill also told me that Herbert was disagreeable on many issues and was an obstacle as a board member. The last thing he needed was for Herbert to come on the administrative staff. My choice scotched the move. Bill argued there was no reason to select outside the hospital since I was a well-qualified internal candidate.

Herbert Lacky remained on the board for a few more years before being replaced. Bill Torrence and Bill Ledford engineered the change. It was a decision that would come back to haunt me years later. Herbert was aware of this scheme and it left a bitter taste in his mouth toward them and apparently toward me too.

At the age of thirty-two, I settled into my new role as the assistant administrator. The entire senior management team, including me, consisted of four individuals. Administrator Bill Torrence dealt with all medical staff issues directly. The medical staff governed itself separately, but Bill ensured they adhered to hospital policies and procedures. Howard Kuhns handled finances; Eunice Magee oversaw nursing services; and I was responsible for the ancillary and service departments.

Bill Torrence was my mentor, allowing me the opportunity to learn not only all the aspects of the departments that reported to me but also the interworking of the medical staff. Howard Kuhns educated me on financials, and Eunice Magee tutored me on nursing issues. Those early years were the best, and I learned a lot.

Bill tasked me with other significant duties as well. I served as the hospital's risk and safety manager and coordinated litigation with the hospital attorney. I also served as the hospital's government affairs liaison. In this role, I engaged politicians on the local, state, and federal levels.

At once, Bill threw me into the political fray. Within a few months of my appointment, he had me go before the county commission to present a small hospital construction project for approval. I stumbled through the presentation and took tough questions from a pair of skeptics. These two county commissioners often opposed hospital requests. Finally, I got approval with the help of Bill Ledford. He had become my friend and ally too. Before the meeting, Bill told me not to worry;

he already had the votes lined up to pass the approval motion.

In Bill Torrence, I found a likeminded individual. He was always honest, straightforward, and decisive in his dealings with the medical and hospital staff, the Board of Trustees, politicians, and community leaders. Some criticized Bill for being blunt and unyielding. Still, he had everyone's respect and kept the hospital's best interest at heart.

Bill was particularly critical of our crosstown rival, the one-hundred-bed Cleveland Community Hospital. He did not like its administrator, Jim Whitlock, nor did he like for-profit hospitals in general. At that time, Hospital Corporation of America (HCA), a hospital chain based in Nashville, Tennessee, owned that hospital.

"Before Cleveland Community admits a patient, it performs a wallet biopsy," Bill once told me.

"What's a wallet biopsy?"

"It's when they open your billfold to see if you can pay before treating you." Bill laughed. "Whitlock and I don't get along very well. We've had a few knock-down, drag-out fights through the years over lots of issues. He recruits competing doctors we don't need. But there are times when he does bring in a good one. I let him do it, and then woo that doctor to start practicing here at Bradley Memorial. At Cleveland Community Hospital, vendors say they have to put money under the table before getting money over the table."

"Who are they talking about, Bill?"

"I'm not saying, but that's what they tell me."

Bill Torrence consistently backed me up on any decision I made. One of the first instructions he gave me regarded being the administrator on call.

"Michael, when the house supervisor calls you about an issue, they're looking for an answer. They want you to make the decision; so make it. Now later, we can discuss what you decided, and I'll give you my opinion. But even if I disagree, I'll back you up."

Bill Torrence's support made my decision-making much more manageable.

The four senior managers rotated the administrator-on-call role, each serving for an entire week, twenty-four hours a day, once a month. I carried a beeper and stuffed my pockets with plenty of quarters for payphones.

Early on, I also faced an ethical challenge that defined how I would handle such issues in the future. You can teach a person ethics, but such training does not ensure they have integrity because ethical behavior goes to the core of a person's being. It reflects their character.

For me, the opportunity came from an insurance agent. He came to my office requesting that we include his products in our benefits package for employees. Such plans required voluntary participation from employees with no employer match. They consisted of certain types of dental, life, and cancer insurance programs. We already offered these products through a different company. The insurance representative wanted to replace them with his. I carefully reviewed our current plans and compared them to his company's. They were virtually identical.

"No," I told him. "I see no need to switch since you offer essentially the same products—just a different insurance company. Even the premiums are almost identical."

"I see. What can I do to convince you?" the agent responded.

"Nothing. I've made my decision."

"Okay," he replied. "I know what you want." He took out a note-pad and pen and began scribbling something. I could see he was calculating figures. Finally, he said, "Based on my estimate of total sales, I can offer you thirty thousand dollars. How does that sound?"

The insurance agent was offering me a kickback. As a county employee, it was illegal for me to accept such an offer. I was shocked. I was outraged. It was the last thing I had expected. I sat and stared at the man in disbelief, trying to process what he had just said.

I stood up over my desk; he was sitting on the other side.

"Get out of my office and never come back to this hospital again! Do I make myself clear?"

The agent, clearly shaken and trembling with anger, did not say a word. He left at once.

❖ ❖ ❖

Work at the hospital went smoothly for the next few years. I took on volunteer leadership roles with the United Way and the Chamber of Commerce and joined the Kiwanis Club. These roles not only benefited the hospital but also embedded me in the community. I got deeply involved in politics. It was this role that allowed me to become a considerable political force within the hospital and the broader community over time.

Part of my journey in this career path was getting public recognition. In January 1986, I was given the Cleveland Jaycee's Distinguished Service Award as an Outstanding Young Business Leader. Twice, the *Cleveland Daily Banner* ran front-page personality profiles on my accomplishments.

I never overthought about my future at Bradley Memorial Hospital. I imagined I would have to work there several years to get the required experience to advance. Some believed Bill Torrence was grooming me to succeed him as the administrator, but we never discussed the idea. The Board of Trustees was as much a political group as a governing body. I knew politics would play a heavy hand in selecting a replacement for Bill Torrence when the time came. Bill's announcement of his early retirement made this prospect a reality.

Bill Torrence's decision to retire centered around an outpatient radiology building built on the hospital campus's western corner. By the late 1980s, outpatient services were cropping up as an alternative to hospitals' more expensive in-house services. Our hospital-based radiology group demanded Bradley Memorial Hospital take steps to prevent competition. If another radiology group opened an outpatient facility, it would drain revenue away from them. The board approved the plan, which was seen as a fantastic way to discourage these competitors while providing new, state-of-the-art outpatient radiology services to the community. I went to the county commission and got approval. There was no known opposition from the medical community.

Work on the facility began routinely, but rumblings surfaced somewhere during the construction phase. Resistance developed from doctors associated with Cleveland Community Hospital. Such disapproval from these players seemed familiar. When the issue of obtaining a Certificate of Need (CON) came up for discussion, Bill Torrence rebutted the need. He viewed the facility as an extension of hospital services, which did not require approval.

A Certificate of Need is a legal document required by many states, including Tennessee, before a hospital can add new or expand existing services. Neither construction nor the offering of services can begin before the CON is issued. The central idea of requiring CONs is the claim that overbuilding and redundancy in the provision of healthcare services leads to higher costs. Not obtaining a Certificate of Need could have an adverse outcome for a hospital, leading to the new facility or service shutting down.

The new outpatient building opened among these swirling arguments. To augment the idea that the new facility was an extension of the services already provided, Bradley Memorial billed inpatient rates. The same billing codes utilized for inpatient radiology services applied to the new outpatient services. The controversy settled down for several months, but it soon resurfaced. Medicare ruled the hospital's billing practices were wrong. They required these radiology procedures to use

outpatient billing codes and charge outpatient rates. The change resulted in less reimbursement and made outpatient services unprofitable.
This change gave new life to those who believed filing a CON should
have happened in the first place. If the hospital was billing for outpatient procedures, the facility must be an outpatient operation requiring
a CON. This explosive news quickly made its way back to Cleveland
Community Hospital. Tensions rose as we waited to see if an aggrieved
party would challenge the new facility.

The following events happened rapidly. Bill Torrence announced
his forthcoming retirement. Howard Kuhns, who was about the same
age as Bill, made it clear that he was not interested in becoming the
administrator. However, the biggest surprise of all was that Jim Whitlock was brought on as an assistant administrator at Bradley Memorial. His duties were to be determined later. To say I was shocked is
an understatement. Neither Bill Torrence nor Howard Kuhns had
brought me into the discussion. Sam Bettis announced Jim's hiring at
the next board meeting.

It was obvious that Bill was choosing to retire because of the
outpatient facility debacle. After Jim Whitlock came to Bradley Memorial, the issue mysteriously disappeared from discussion within the
medical community. I recognized its fading as confirmation of my
suspicion.

Bill was unhappy Jim had joined our administration. He barely
spoke to Jim in the following months leading to his retirement. To
make this point clear, Bill never assigned Jim any duties; just gave
him an office and let him sit. Jim Whitlock was an assistant administrator without a portfolio, a circumstance he blamed on me.

"You wanted to be administrator, and Bill was trying to help you
out," Jim told me later.

When I approached Howard and asked him to explain Jim's hiring, he was evasive but said, "Jim is my friend. I helped him get the

job here, and he is professionally qualified. He'll be our next administrator."

They had set the plan in motion and had not included me in the discussion. After Jim's arrival, I immediately felt his cold shoulder and suspiciousness. Things suddenly looked very bleak. I was not sure I had a future at Bradley Memorial Hospital.

❖ ❖ ❖

After a few months and as Bill's retirement approached, Howard began to have second thoughts about his previous blanket refusal to apply to be the administrator. He had worked at Bradley Memorial for a long time and had many years invested in the institution. He felt it was his duty and his right to become the administrator. He said he would keep the position for only two years, until he reached the typical retirement age.

Howard approached Sam Bettis and other board members about his change of heart. Would they accept it? The answer was yes. Howard Kuhns became the third administrator in the hospital's history. Jim Whitlock was surely disappointed; Howard's deception was profound. However, the knowledge he would only have to wait two more years offered Jim an incentive to stay.

Howard Kuhns assumed the top post of Bradley Memorial Hospital on October 1, 1987. His tenure was chaotic. His management style was opposite that of Bill Torrence, who was always decisive. Howard, on the other hand, could not easily make a choice. He agonized over every decision. Heated, tumultuous debates often broke out. Howard would sometimes overrule himself. It was a terrible environment.

As an example of this behavior, I was given the responsibility of terminating the employment of an individual, which was always one of the more unpleasant duties I occasionally had to perform. I talked at length with Howard to make sure this action was what was needed and what he wanted. After the deed was done, the next day, Howard called me into his office to say he'd changed his mind. The individual had appealed the decision to him personally. Howard felt sorry for the person and had reversed his own decision. In addition to causing chaos and confusion within the department, the reversal also undermined my authority.

The most public example of Howard Kuhns' indecisiveness, however, involved the hospital's switch in blood suppliers. Red Cross had been our provider for decades. Still, when Howard became administrator, the director of Blood Assurance approached him about switching. Blood Assurance was a regional blood bank.

Howard and the director of Blood Assurance had been friends for years. The man had been a hospital administrator in the Chattanooga area for several decades before taking the Blood Assurance job. Howard readily agreed, not thinking through the ramifications. He announced the decision with no notice to Red Cross and no public input.

The change instantly set off a firestorm of opposition from community leaders led by the local Red Cross organization director. Howard received an avalanche of telephone calls from Red Cross board members and other supporters. Concerned citizens and Red Cross supporters inundated the newspaper with calls opposing the move. Howard was on the verge of switching back to the Red Cross. He kept his decision only because many of his advisors at Bradley Memorial, including myself, convinced him not to switch back. It would make him look weak in the public's eye.

I developed a strategy that was somewhat effective in dealing with Howard Kuhns' indecisiveness. One had to be both the first and the last person to talk to Howard to make the decision stick. He usually went with the last word. Understanding Howard's tendency gave me a strategic advantage over others. After addressing an issue, I would wait and watch as others came and went from Howard's office while the matter remained under discussion. When all had had their say, I would return for the last word, to reiterate my position. Then, afterward, I nursed the decision to its implementation.

Howard did not like the strain of line management, where decisions often involved winners and losers. He had spent his entire hospital career in finance and preferred making decisions about numbers that had no human face. Howard was often clueless. Managing department heads and the medical staff was new to him. To compensate, he shifted much of this responsibility to Jim Whitlock. Howard kept his old job but now with the title "administrator."

Howard was very decisive, however, at least once. He shut down the outpatient radiology building shortly after becoming the administrator. The expensive structure with its leaded walls built to shield radiation became the hospital's Department of Human Resources. It was confirmation that failure to get a CON for the project and the potential for acute embarrassment at the end of a storied career was too much. The debacle had led to Bill's retirement. Working out a deal with Jim Whitlock to bring him to Bradley Memorial in exchange for the issue dying and allowing Bill to retire with his reputation intact seemed logical.

After Howard became the administrator, he and Jim began discussing the likelihood of the sale of Bradley Memorial to a bigger hospital system. By the 1980s, the industry was seeing many more acquisitions of smaller healthcare facilities by their competitors or others wanting to expand into a new service area. At the time, Bradley Memorial was performing well. I wondered what interested Howard and Jim in wanting to sell the hospital. They invited representatives from Baptist Hospital of Knoxville down to discuss their interests. The meeting was very secretive.

I got word of the impending visit and contacted Bill Ledford to let him know they were coming.

"They won't sell the hospital as long as I'm on the board. I'll take care of that meeting. Thanks, Michael," Bill said.

It was the first of what became many tipoffs I gave Bill over the years about Jim's efforts to sell Bradley Memorial Hospital. While I saw that such a decision might have to occur sometime in the future, I also believed in full disclosure of such overtures. The entire community should decide. The county commission deserved the opportunity to step up and fund the hospital if they wanted it to remain in local hands. I also knew the present time was not right to sell. There would be too much opposition from the public and county commissioners. I questioned Howard and Jim's motives.

My relationships with Howard and Jim were tenuous. I knew I was in trouble. Jim's attitude toward me was often distrustful and unfriendly, and he routinely questioned my decisions. Howard backed up many of Jim's criticisms. They were setting me up for failure.

Jim once tried to provoke me into a verbal fight. In the exchange, he let me know just how close he and Howard were. "You just need to know Howard Kuhns is my *best* friend."

Howard weighed in, too, suggesting it was time for me to look for another job and denying me a routine raise that had already been approved by the Board of Trustees.

"Your performance is not up to par," is all he said when I asked for an explanation. It was the first criticism of my job performance I had ever heard since coming to the hospital. Bill Torrence always gave me great reviews.

I knew I would have to counteract Howard and Jim's intentions if I was to remain at Bradley Memorial Hospital. I again enlisted the help of Bill Ledford, who was happy to help. I never learned to whom he spoke about me. But Bill called me after a few days and said I shouldn't have any more trouble. He encouraged me not to worry. He said that if I did meet any further opposition, he would take care of it. I never had to call Bill again on the issue, and soon, it felt like I had survived.

CHAPTER
4

Jim Whitlock became the fourth administrator of Bradley Memorial Hospital at the beginning of 1990. His ascension was a foregone conclusion following Howard Kuhns' retirement. The Board of Trustees did conduct a cursory candidate search, and several local candidates, including hospital employees, applied. I was not one of them, presuming that Jim already had the position. Howard Kuhns asked me to keep a file on each candidate and send copies to board members. They selected Jim at their next meeting.

Among the seven board members at the time of Jim Whitlock's appointment were Sam Bettis, who served as chairman, Bob Sain, and Bill Ledford.

In coordination with Sam Bettis, these seven members supplied a perfect rubber stamp board. A rubber stamp board takes a hands-off approach to its duties. It simply approves everything put in front of it with little or no deliberation or debate. This board was controlled entirely in the early years by Bill Torrence, then by Howard Kuhns, and finally by Jim Whitlock.

After Jim became the administrator of Bradley Memorial, he set about restructuring the hospital's management to suit him. Jim's first act was to secure the resignation of the hospital's CPA, who had clashed with him from the time of his arrival. Howard Kuhns and the CPA had together functioned as the de facto CFO. In their place, Jim hired Craig Taylor as the new CPA and elevated that position to CFO.

Craig was young and inexperienced when he came to Bradley Memorial. However, his freshness allowed Jim to train Craig to his liking. He became a total ally of Jim Whitlock, never taking a step without Jim's blessing.

Jim set about broadening senior management to include various individuals who could serve as sounding boards about operational and strategic initiatives. Initially, there were seven individuals, including Jim, which later expanded to nine. Most of them became totally devoted to Jim and his leadership.

I was a member of this senior management group. Jim must have felt stuck with me since his earlier attempt to oust me had failed. By the time he became the administrator, I had strengthened my ties to the political establishment. I expanded my network to include many other county commissioners besides Bill Ledford, including a host of other local elected officials. I worked in campaigns, donated money, and attended rallies. These activities were a genuine interest on my part. Still, I knew the deeper I immersed myself in the community's political fabric, the more difficult it would be for Jim to touch me.

Of the group, the nursing director and I oversaw the most employees. The nursing department composed around sixty percent of the entire hospital staff, roughly six hundred employees. The ancillary and service departments that I directed were next with over 275 workers. I had seven department heads reporting directly to me.

All the other senior managers split the remaining 125 employees among themselves. They filled prominent roles as senior managers, considering how few people they oversaw. How many departments and employees each senior manager supervised became a source of friction and contention as the years passed under Jim's executive model. I often had to fend off people's attempts to take my departments. Human resources was one of only a few that I lost, but that was a necessary change after its director became a senior manager. He reported directly to Jim.

Jealously also arose from those who did not have the title of assistant administrator toward those who did. In the early days, many lobbied Jim to give them the title too, but wary of bestowing the title on too many people, he was reluctant. He finally said everyone should be satisfied with being a senior manager regardless of title.

Weekly meetings of the senior management team occurred on Tuesdays. They usually lasted half a day, sometimes longer. The interactions were freewheeling, chaotic, and dysfunctional. I hated these meetings; they accomplished nothing. Jim must have felt comfortable in such a decision-making model, but I could not see its benefit. It was plausible that Jim's main attraction was the accolades many of these senior managers showered on him at these assemblies. I knew from my time working under Bill Torrence that his four senior managers working together coordinating separate duties were very efficient. Bill Torrence's group did more than Jim's assemblage could have ever dreamed of doing.

Groupthink invariably took over. Creative thinking and individual responsibility gave way to group consensus. In discussing an issue, senior managers often set aside their own beliefs to adopt the rest of the group's opinion.

I was very aware of this phenomenon. As one who tended to oppose the group's decisions and sometimes sought to override their views, I often found myself in a minority position. Over time, I realized that I would find myself in trouble if I did not moderate my interactions with the group. In the early years, I remained quiet on many issues, choosing to keep the peace and avoid disrupting the group's dynamics. I limited my opposition, saving it for the issues I felt strongest about.

Later, as the hospital's financial situation deteriorated, I felt compelled to speak up more often and oppose many decisions. Groupthink became a critical dynamic in my colleagues' negative views of me.

Jim did not bring all issues to the weekly senior management meetings, keeping some under his direct control and making his own decisions. One example is hospital bidding practices. Shortly after becoming the administrator, Jim directed me to start buying all our office goods from a certain company. When I protested that we should first bid for the best price, Jim reluctantly agreed. I instructed our director of materials management to send out proposals. When we got them back, our current supplier had the lowest bid. After his review, Jim told me to award the contract to the other company anyway because the owner was his "good friend." He also moved the director of materials management directly under his control, which cut me out of any future bid decision-making.

Construction project bidding was another area Jim tightly controlled. Sam Bettis and Jim always opened and awarded the bids. After one such session, one contractor came into my office disgruntled.

"You can't ever get any work here unless you're willing to pay something first," the contractor said.

"You know I don't have anything to do with bidding construction projects."

"I know. I'm just expressing my frustrations."

❖ ❖ ❖

When Jim Whitlock became the administrator, he set out immediately to increase hospital revenue. To achieve this goal, he instructed CFO Craig Taylor to raise charges for all patient items and services. The hospital was extraordinarily aggressive in its pricing and amazingly successful. At first, insurers did not balk at these price in-

creases because our fees had historically been very low. They interpreted these increases as the hospital's catching up to more current
rates. Over the next several years, Bradley Memorial Hospital went
from being the lowest-cost provider in the region to one of the highest.

Unlike Bill Torrence, Jim saw working capital as the key ingredi-
ent to the hospital's future. He was not afraid to increase cash reserves
to levels Bill would have feared. Jim rightly concluded that the public
and county commission had forgotten the earlier fight over which entity should control the funds. Jim appeared a miracle worker for the
unsuspecting public, our board members, and most senior managers.

Over the next few years, using this tactic of aggressively increasing charges, he turned the hospital into a tremendous success. Hospital financial reports glowed as they showed strong upward trends.
Many community leaders welcomed the progress of the hospital.

Marketing and Public Relations Director Dewayne Belew,
a member of the senior management team, built up the hospital's
achievements through the press. Dewayne was good at his job and
one of the most ardent supporters of Jim among our group. He crafted a compelling image of the hospital and of Jim Whitlock for the
public. Silently ambitious and cunning, Dewayne wanted to ride
Jim's coattails as far as they would take him.

Jim became a featured speaker before civic and industrial leaders, community organizations, and politicians. Throughout the early
1990s, it looked as if Bradley Memorial Hospital was succeeding beyond everyone's highest expectations.

Coupled with this financial success, Bradley Memorial became
one of the top hundred hospitals in America in 1994. The achievement came through a study, Benchmarks for Success. In 1995, the
hospital received an honorable mention in the same study. It was a
prestigious award and a stunning achievement that Dewayne and Jim

set out at once to exploit in the public's eye. Bradley's goodwill soared as praises poured in from the community and healthcare industry peers.

The hospital's marketing and public relations efforts exaggerated the hospital's healthcare quality. Ads ran for more than two years, hailing this success. But things were not exactly as they appeared. Conveniently omitted was one crucial detail. The information analyzed was financial data, not quality data. It came from the time Bill Torrence was the administrator when Bradley Memorial was the lowest-cost provider in the region. The Top 100 Hospital award was not Jim's at all. That point, however, did not keep Jim from exploiting it to his advantage.

❖ ❖ ❖

As revenue started increasing, Bradley Memorial began a thirty-million-dollar building project. It required us taking on a substantial debt for a mid-sized rural hospital, made possible by the hospital's improved financial status. Phase one of this plan included the addition of two floors atop the existing patient tower. The new fourth floor had patient rooms and an endoscopy unit, and the new fifth floor had an outpatient surgery center and a pediatrics unit. Phase one also included renovations to older patient areas and the emergency room, enhancements to the imaging facilities, and a new cardiopulmonary suite.

Phase two of the hospital's building plan totaled twenty-two million dollars. It included an ambitious medical mall that housed outpatient registration on the first level, a gift shop, and a chapel. Also located on this first level was a new obstetrics center. Windows lined the mall to allow onlookers to see into the nursery.

The lower level had dining facilities, including a food court for the public and employees. The hospital's dietary service ran this operation in addition to supplying inpatient food services. There was also space on the lower level for an educational facility and a public auditorium.

On the second floor of the mall was a new executive office suite that included a board room, where large sliding glass doors opened to a balcony that overlooked the entire glass-roofed structure. Jim's office was vast. He spent hundreds of thousands of dollars on the new executive suite. Some of the senior managers, including me, also occupied space in the offices next to Jim. A central secretarial area connected all of us. Other senior manager offices were off the main suite, through a hidden door off the hallway. A glass elevator allowed access from the executive office suite to the areas below.

Renovation of the patient tower's older third floor was part of phase two. It also included a new parking garage to satisfy growing parking needs. It also happens that this was the first parking garage ever built in Cleveland. The hospital first had to buy and demolish an adjoining small, two-story physician office building to make room.

To accommodate his top interest, Sam Bettis insisted the hospital build a new external power plant facility on the western end of the campus to house all utilities. The project included a full-length tunnel and not merely a chase. Stretching from a service elevator found under the hospital's basement, it traversed west beneath the parking lot for about the length of a football field. It allowed utilities to connect to the hospital and gave maintenance and engineering employees easy access back and forth along the hallway.

By the end of phase two construction, Bradley Memorial Hospital's finances began to feel the strain. However, Jim Whitlock still wanted to construct more buildings. He was particularly interested in a new, modern medical office building. It would be an attraction for new physician recruitment and help keep established physicians nearby. In 1996, with this strategy in mind, he embarked on a new effort to buy the vacant property to the south of the hospital's campus and build a large four-story medical office building.

Initially, Jim took the plan to the Bradley County Commission for approval. Because of the cost of acquiring the land, development, and building the structure, the county commission denied the hospital's request. It was the first time since Bill Ledford's election to the county commission that he had suffered a defeat on a hospital issue.

Not willing to take no for an answer, Jim devised an alternate plan. With the Board of Trustees' approval, Jim set up a joint venture known as Bradley Building. It was done very quietly and out of the public's eye. Neither the press nor county commission representatives were in attendance when the board approved the plan. Jim recruited a local commercial development company, Joe Rogers & Associates, as a partner to construct the building and Southeast Venture Corporation to provide architectural and interior design. When Bradley Building announced these plans, virtually no one in the community knew who controlled this group.

Bradley Memorial owned seventy-five percent of the partnership. Joe Rogers & Associates and Southeast Venture Corporation shared the other twenty-five percent. The hospital used its credit rating to secure an 8.5-million-dollar loan from SunTrust Bank. The loan allowed Bradley Building to buy the land and begin construction on the multi-million-dollar facility.

Jim believed all the hospital's construction projects, including this new medical office building, supplied needed improvements, positioned the hospital to be competitive in the future, and would be paid for by a continuous stream of new revenue.

❖ ❖ ❖

Jim used these construction projects as factors to motivate the community, physicians, and hospital staff, but he also wished to inspire his managers in other ways. He emphasized teambuilding, first with the senior managers and later with department heads and nurse managers.

Jim spent inordinate hours with senior managers, both in the weekly administration meetings and social activities. No one dared skip any of it. The idea was the more time we spent together, getting to know each other, the better we would trust one another. We also began holding annual two-day senior management retreats away from the hospital.

As part of what Jim described as helping to "establish new trust," we had to bring all our significant decisions to the Tuesday meetings for discussion and approval. Many of these deliberations became lively and sometimes heated as each player staked out positions that favored their areas of control. Because most wanted Jim's support, they looked for signs of how he was weighing an issue and began moving their positions closer to his. Regardless of the case, we all knew that only Jim's vote counted even though we had a say.

The approach unnecessarily bogged down hospital operations. Decisions languished while awaiting approval.

Once Jim felt he had control of senior managers, he extended his teambuilding approach to lower-ranking hospital managers. We held three-day off-campus retreats each year. Senior managers used presentations, teambuilding exercises, and lots of social activities to win support. Senior managers conducted various skits to help drive home the theme for that year's retreat and give directors and nurse managers a glimpse of their humor. The hospital planned annual board retreats for the same purpose, as well as to get members' input on its strategic plan.

We held these retreats for many years. We had meetings in Gatlinburg and Fairfield Glade in Tennessee and Brasstown Valley, Georgia, which became the favored location. All the senior managers, department heads, nurse managers, and board members looked forward to these events. They were more like parties, filled with golf, hiking, shopping, relaxing, and many other activities.

Customer service—or "guest excellence," as Jim labeled it—also became a significant initiative. It was not about improving the quality of care but about being friendly to guests and making them feel like hospital staff cared. The program began with a "mystery patient" who checked himself into the hospital under an assumed name with the help of a select few nurses and a physician. During his stay, this individual simply watched his treatment by the staff and kept notes.

After his discharge, Dave Gordon presented his findings to senior managers, department heads, and nurse managers. He was mostly complimentary about the care he'd received. Dave was a consultant who had been a mystery patient many times at other hospitals and offered training to improve how employees interacted with patients. The mystery patient's focus was to emphasize the idea that there were dividends to treating patients with respect. After Dave's stay, the hospital administration established a task force to develop employee recognition and rewards. Dave Gordon stayed on as a consultant supplying training to every hospital employee.

Task force members believed Dave Gordon was amazingly useful. Still, some hospital employees thought his training was a waste of time. When I asked one staff member what they had learned in Dave's class, he replied sarcastically, "Well, he told us when asked how we're doing to say, 'Terrific!'"

When making my rounds through the hospital, I began asking this question to see what response I would get.

"How are you today?"

"Terrific!" was often the smiling, mocking response.

To assess the hospital's teambuilding and guest excellence programs, Jim hired Zimmerman & Associates from Milwaukee, Wisconsin. Their mission was to conduct a study of Bradley Memorial Hospital's approach.

David Zimmerman published his findings of Bradley Memorial in his 1996 book, *The Healthcare Customer Service Revolution.* This over-the-top account heaped high praise and various accolades on Jim Whitlock's success at Bradley Memorial Hospital.

The need for recognition was Jim Whitlock's primary motivation for all these team-building and guest excellence efforts because, at best, they were only marginally successful. But these changes satisfied Jim's apparent need for admiration and appreciation from the hospital staff. They also helped him become known in the healthcare industry as an innovative leader.

Jim's efforts worked. He became Chairman of the Tennessee Hospital Association (THA) Board of Trustees.

CHAPTER
5

By the end of the hospital's phase two construction project, it appeared Bradley Memorial was headed for prestige among the annals of healthcare. The hospital had also climbed atop the list of high-cost providers in the region. It had achieved this lofty perch through annual, aggressive increases in its patient charges. In the early years, insurance companies had overlooked its practice of forceful price increases because the hospital had been an extremely low-cost provider. The insurance companies believed Bradley Memorial was simply catching up. Eventually, they began pushing back, negotiating more favorable contractual allowances for its patients. Medicare and Medicaid used non-negotiable contractual allowances, but these federally regulated adjustments had always been a part of the hospital's revenue projection.

A contractual allowance or adjustment is the difference between what a hospital bills for services versus what they will receive based on its contract with an insurer or the government. The reimbursement amount is always lower than the billed amount.

Bradley Memorial was in a weak negotiating position. Cross-town rival Cleveland Community Hospital was ready and willing to accept more patients if our negotiations broke down. Losing even one of these insurance companies' provider networks would have proven financially disastrous for the hospital. As a result, Bradley Memorial accepted these lower payments. Moving forward, the hospital grew much more slowly in its patient revenue. Bradley Memorial's tactic of raising patient charges to increase revenue had ended.

To boost revenue, Jim Whitlock and Craig Taylor brought in the Ramsey Group, a consulting firm, to help configure ways to increase revenue. Upcoding techniques seemed to offer the best solution. Upcoding occurs when a hospital bills medical codes for more serious, more expensive diagnoses or procedures than they diagnose or preform. Medical coding transforms hospital diagnoses, procedures, medical services, and medical equipment into alphanumeric codes for billing purposes. Upcoding results in overcharges for these services.

Such consultants' careers were flourishing because many hospitals were struggling financially and trying to improve revenue. These coding experts could sometimes dramatically increase hospital profits. They typically signed prospective, contingency-basis contracts, which was the case with the Ramsey Group.

The Ramsey Group's professional fees were fifty percent of any additional revenue from their inpatient coding assessment of specific types of Medicare record samples, such as pneumonia. They also received fifty percent of the additional annualized revenue from their outpatient coding assessments of randomly chosen ambulatory surgery records samples. If there were no revenue enhancements from these specific and random records, the hospital owed nothing except the out-of-pocket expenses that consisted primarily of travel costs. The contract stipulated that the Ramsey Group bill these expenditures to Bradley Memorial at their cost. There was a negligible risk for these consulting groups. They could always find diagnoses to be upcoded.

These companies made a lot of money until Medicare officials ruled prospective, contingency reimbursement schemes illegal. Such arrangements then became the focus of Medicare investigators.

Bradley Memorial's first clinical coding enhancement agreement with the Ramsey Group was so successful that CFO Craig Taylor signed an amended contract that allowed for much more aggressive inpatient coding. The hospital agreed to a one-hundred-percent review of the records. It also reduced the Ramsey Group's professional fees to 33.3 percent. But, for them, this change still meant more revenue because more accounts were subject to review, even though their overall professional fee percentage went down.

When providers upcode medical bills for Medicare or Medicaid patients, they defraud the government and all taxpayers, as taxes pay for these overcharges. It became a grave issue at Bradley Memorial Hospital. Pneumonia upcoding was particularly flagrant, but it was not the only one.

Medicare began scrutinizing hospitals and other healthcare providers across the country. States launched parallel investigations over Medicaid billing. Hospitals began shedding their upcoding consultants and hoped they would avoid detection or braced themselves for what was to come. It was in this environment that Bradley Memorial entered the late 1990s. These schemes, along with growing financial strain, created significant challenges as Bradley Memorial Hospital moved toward the turn of the century.

Flat revenue growth following a decadelong aggressive building program spelled trouble ahead for the hospital as it began to repay revenue bonds issued for construction.

I had many concerns about all the building activity during those years. I did not verbalize my disapproval because I felt my opinion would not have mattered due to groupthink. No one else saw the folly of what the hospital was doing. I remained silent, keeping my opinions to myself.

In my view, much of the new construction was unnecessary. Only a small part of it helped patient care. Some developments, such as the obstetrics and pediatrics departments, focused on services that lost money, even if they were important. Other improvements, like imaging and emergency room services, were only cosmetic, focusing on new paint, lighting, and flooring while adding no new patient equipment. Twenty-year-old beds and stretchers and thirty-year-old radiographic equipment remained in use.

The plan included new patient rooms, but it excluded a new and much needed surgical suite. Jim was more interested in aesthetics on the newly constructed fourth and fifth floors and the renovated third floor. He directed the laying of carpet in the hallways. The carpet did not last long. It was challenging to roll hospital equipment and wheelchairs over the surface. Physicians cultured samples of the carpet to discover unwanted and dangerous pathogens. Tile eventually replaced the carpet.

The new external power plant facility and its connecting tunnel were grossly unnecessary. The parking garage solved a problem, but not at the expense of buying and demolishing a medical office building. The executive office suite, glass elevator, food court, educational facility, and auditorium were wasteful additions.

Even the beautiful glass ceiling in the medical mall added nothing to patient care. Jim insisted the flooring of the mall include an expensive slate tile. While it was attractive, the flooring's rough surface made it almost impossible for wheelchairs to cross. It required a change to allow for most patient discharges to occur at the east exit.

Jim also wanted to add an aviary along the top of the medical mall's glass ceiling, a shameless luxury and an outrageous notion. The idea progressed until I protested and produced evidence that Tennessee regulations prohibited them in medical facilities.

Forming Bradley Building, silently and in direct defiance of the county commission, to build a new four-story medical office building was political and financial madness. Once completed, it meant hundreds of thousands of dollars in future revenue went to annual lease payments, which soon became a crippling drain on Bradley Memorial's finances.

Initiatives like teambuilding and guest excellence, whose importance paled in comparison to repaying revenue bonds and lease payments, were also considerably expensive. Over the years, the hospital spent tens of thousands of dollars on retreats for senior managers, department heads, nurse managers, and board members. Dave Gordon commanded ten thousand dollars a week to train employees in guest excellence. In addition to thousands of dollars of consulting fees paid to Dave Zimmerman, the hospital bought hundreds of copies of his book. This bulk sale helped it move up on the healthcare bestseller list. Jim gave a copy to every hospital employee. Even after that, there were many books left over. They went to storage and there they stayed.

As more hospitals came under review by Medicare officials for their upcoding strategies, Jim Whitlock began to pay attention. In 1996, Jim, Craig, the nursing director, and I attended an educational program to learn about the types of diagnoses federal officials were investigating. We were also there to find out what other hospitals were doing to prepare for Medicare's scrutiny. Jim's response was to act unconcerned. Craig downplayed the seriousness of the issue for Bradley Memorial. The nursing director and I did not know what to think, as the meeting was our introduction to the subject. I had only read about the issue in trade magazines, so it seemed far away at the time.

Notwithstanding Jim's and Craig's indifferent appearance, they signed a contract with Compliance Concepts, Inc., to review the hospital's billing practices. Their evaluation continued throughout 1997.

CHAPTER
6

During these years, overtures to healthcare companies interested in buying the hospital continued. When it came to selling the hospital, Jim Whitlock was a maniac. He went from the highest high when the prospects were good to the lowest low when there was no progress. Jim brought his senior managers along on these teeter-totter rides. Their moods rose and fell along with his. Some contacts with potential buyers were overt, while others were covert. Whichever they were, I knew about most of them and contacted Bill Ledford to let him know. Bill continued to thwart these efforts.

The most significant public attempt to buy Bradley Memorial Hospital came in 1996 from Erlanger Health System. Erlanger was a tertiary public hospital found in nearby Chattanooga, Tennessee. Jim had met with Erlanger officials privately to discuss the prospects. He was moving slowly to warm the Board of Trustees to the idea. Jim also welcomed overtures from for-profits Columbia/HCA and Community Health Systems. Still, because the hospital was public, it seemed Erlanger's offered the best chance of success with the Board of Trustees, the county commission, and the community.

Before Jim's efforts could progress, however, County Executive Donna Hubbard's proposal exploded in the local press. She had been negotiating separately with Erlanger officials and announced the deal at the Board of Trustees meeting on September 10, 1996.

Donna was a Democrat in a solidly Republican county. I had a personal connection with Donna Hubbard. I considered her a friend. When I first returned to Cleveland after grad school, I lived next-door to Donna and her family. Later, we also attended church together.

Many believed Donna's first election in 1986 was a fluke, the result of a lazy incumbent. The Republican, Eddie Cartwright, was running for reelection. Donna won the Democratic primary. I was skeptical—not because she was female, but because she had no prior political experience. Eddie was so confident of defeating a woman that he did not campaign, staying put in his office at the courthouse throughout the campaign. Donna, by contrast, fought hard all over the county. She styled herself as a populist and the candidate of working people. Eddie's misogynistic strategy backfired. Donna beat him soundly and began serving her first term. After her win, Donna asked if I would be interested in leaving my hospital position to work for her. I declined, believing the hospital to be a much more excellent opportunity.

The overconfident, sexist attitude from her opponents continued during Donna Hubbard's reelections of 1990 and 1994.

Jim Sharp, a wealthy developer, opposed her in 1990. Donna exploited Jim's riches, chauvinistic tendencies, and dislike by local realtors, and she defeated him by a comfortable margin. Realtors opposed Jim because his Sharp Developments bypassed them, selling building lots directly to buyers.

I sensed Jim Sharp's weakness and laid some preliminary plans to oppose him in the primary. I believed winning a political office might be preferable to staying at Bradley Memorial with an uncertain future under Jim Whitlock. I recruited a high-ranking industrial leader to serve as my campaign treasurer in the event I decided to run.

Jim Sharps' response was to lean on both of us, to force me out of the race. Jim Sharp met with Jim Whitlock to express his displeasure. He then met with me to discuss the race. I told Jim Sharp he was an unpopular, vulnerable candidate, and he could not defeat Donna Hubbard. He did not like my comments.

Jim Sharp then recruited several key business leaders to put the pressure on my would-be treasurer. Jim Sharp and his allies convinced him to withdraw from my fledgling effort. Without a top-notch campaign fundraiser, I dropped the idea, but not before incurring the wrath of Jim Sharp. From then on, Jim Sharp was never supportive of any of my political ventures. He stayed a constant source of opposition even after I became Chairman of the Bradley County Republican Party.

Donna Hubbard was also upset. She could not understand why I would even entertain the idea of running against her. I pointed out various controversial positions Donna had taken that would make her vulnerable if the Republicans chose the right candidate.

"If you want to run against me," she scolded, "come on and do it. I'll welcome the competition."

I was right about Jim Sharp. In the Republican primary, he defeated a little-known candidate by an uncomfortably close margin, a precursor of his defeat in the general election.

In 1994, Donna's opponent was Louie Alford, a retired coach and educator. In the primary, Louie went up against County Commissioner Gary Davis and a local reporter. The reporter siphoned enough votes away from Gary's existing base of supporters to ensure Louie's primary victory. Like Eddie Cartwright, Louie Alford also did not believe a woman could beat him, making smirky remarks about Donna's gender on the campaign trail. The result was another loss, the same as Eddie Cartwright and Jim Sharp before him.

These wins against what seemed to be impossible odds turned

Donna Hubbard into a steely, hardnosed county executive. All her proposals met opposition from the supermajority Republican county commission. Donna's counterstrategy was to go to the public to rally her supporters. She was tenacious, never giving up. For Donna, there were no failures, only setbacks. Her disdain for the community elite extended beyond the county commission to other institutions, including Bradley Memorial Hospital.

Donna did not like Jim Whitlock and was always suspicious and hostile toward him. I never understood the source of her hatred. She thought Bill Ledford's membership on the hospital's Board of Trustees was a conflict of interest. He was an elected member of the county commission, its oversight body. By 1996, Bill was Chairman of the Bradley County Commission, making him an even bigger target for Donna.

County Executive Hubbard believed Bradley County would be better off if it sold the hospital and used the profits for much-needed school improvements. Erlanger cautiously backed Donna's proposal but said its only interest in Bradley Memorial was as an ally on hand to defeat investor-owned health systems' offers. But if Erlanger officials initially thought teaming up with Donna was a good strategy, they soon recognized their folly.

Donna's announcement of the deal to the hospital's Board of Trustees set off a whirlwind of news coverage, political debate, public discourse, and employee upheaval. Her goal was simple—ask the fourteen elected members of the Bradley County Commission to sell Bradley Memorial. The county would get an estimated ninety million dollars from the region's largest healthcare system. The sale would fund seventy million dollars in county education improvements without a property tax hike. According to Donna's plan, the rest of the money could supply a perpetual fund for the county, which would allow it to meet state-mandated obligations for local education into the future. She planned to present the proposal quickly, on September 16, 1996, to the county commission for approval.

Donna said her proposal would give the county everything it wanted, including adequate funds for education with no property tax increase and a public hospital. She had secured assurances from Erlanger that Bradley Memorial would continue to have a local board. They would protect the hospital's workforce, keep a strong commitment to indigent care, and commit to enhancing the hospital's level of service.

Donna felt that the county had no choice. The state had passed a law mandating the county invest more than seventy million dollars in schools over the next several years. Without the hospital sale, residents would get a property tax increase of $1.51 on each thousand dollars of their property's assessed value, the first property tax increase in Bradley County since 1987.

The backlash was swift from the Board of Trustees. In a written response, board members unanimously said, "We are opposed to selling Bradley Memorial to Erlanger or anyone." They went on to say, "Our community should not have to choose between its public hospital and its education system. We should not sacrifice one for the other."

The board appointed Jim Whitlock to serve as the hospital's sole spokesperson during all media interviews. He had to oppose the arrangement publicly, a plan Jim had supported privately.

I recognized the hospital would need to conduct its opposition as a political campaign. There were only fourteen votes, those of the fourteen county commissioners, and we needed eight votes to win. I organized the campaign. Dewayne Belew helped me execute it. We mobilized and instructed hospital department heads and supervisors. We appointed team leaders and assigned them specific responsibilities. We started a petition drive resulting in eight thousand, two hundred and twenty signatures (ten percent of the county's population) in less than three days. We planned a march to the courthouse. We began a full-scale telephone assault. Employees and members of the public inundated county commissioners and the county executive's office with calls opposing the sale.

We organized opposition from business and industry and community leaders. The Bradley Healthcare Foundation coordinated the effort. Established after Jim became Bradley Memorial's administrator, its purpose was to raise money for hospital capital projects. Now it weighed in to help defeat Donna Hubbard's proposal. The foundation's board publicly endorsed the hospital and worked diligently to kill the plan. Dewayne organized a media blitz to saturate the coverage with opposition to Donna Hubbard's proposal. We enlisted the help of the Bradley County Medical Society, resulting in one hundred percent opposition.

On the day of the meeting, Bradley County Commission Chairman Bill Ledford got the petition. By the time the county commission meeting started, the room was standing-room-only; the hallways leading from the chamber were also filled. In her presentation, County Executive Hubbard reiterated the need for the sale. The funds would be used for education funding forestalling a tax increase while also preserving Bradley Memorial as a public hospital. Afterward, a commissioner moved not to sell or lease the hospital to any organization. A second quickly followed. After the roll call, the motion passed twelve to zero with two abstentions. Donna's proposal died a quick death.

On the day before the vote, the *Cleveland Daily Banner* ran an unscientific survey question for citizens to complete and send to a Cleveland-based CPA. The paper asked whether citizens were in favor of or against selling the hospital. After tabulations came in, the results showed ninety-three percent of those who completed the ballot opposed to the sale. It was an endorsement of all our efforts.

The Board of Trustees recognized Dewayne Belew and me for our work to stymy the hospital's sale. In the spring of 1997, at the board's annual retreat, Dewayne received the Chairman's Award for Excellence, while I got the Administrator's Award for Excellence. Dewayne began fancying himself a great political strategist. It was an assumption that later cost Bradley Memorial dearly.

Donna Hubbard took the defeat badly. To the newspapers, she denounced the hospital board and the county commission and railed that their decision meant a tax increase for every Bradley Countian.

Still, Donna did not give up. She sought a ruling from the Tennessee Attorney General on the legality of a member of the county commission, in his oversight role, serving on a board he was overseeing. The attorney general's opinion concluded it was illegal, forcing Bill's resignation.

The hospital won the battle but lost an asset in Bill Ledford. While I, too, had lost an important ally on the hospital board with the ruling, I gained another. Gary Davis replaced Bill. He was laying plans to run again for county executive. Gary became a friend and ally.

I never knew what Jim Whitlock's motives were in making these mostly private overtures to parties interested in buying Bradley Memorial Hospital. Jim may have believed it was in the best interest of the community for the hospital to team up with a partner.

I did once hear a consultant hired by the Bradley Healthcare Foundation speak of his own motive. One method for fundraising he suggested was to sell the hospital, place the leftover funds in the foundation, and disburse them for health-related purposes. As the CEO of a healthcare system, the consultant said he'd successfully negotiated its sale to a larger organization. Funds from the sale went to a foundation. He went on to say that he enriched himself from the sale. He received a "finder's fee" from the buyer worth millions of dollars. A finder's fee is a commission paid to a facilitator of a transaction. The intermediary gets the payment for discovering the deal and bringing it to the interested parties' attention.

❖ ❖ ❖

My involvement in defeating Donna Hubbard's attempt to sell Bradley Memorial Hospital was just an extension of my more significant political role in the community. In 1991, I began serving as the Chairman of the Bradley County Republican Party. It was an influential, elected position that allowed me access to every local campaign. I worked in this office until 1997, except for part of 1992, when I resigned to run for the twenty-second district state representative seat.

For my campaign, I got assurances from Jim Whitlock and Sam Bettis that they would accommodate my schedule if I were chosen for the part-time state position. They saw a benefit to the hospital. I was not sure I trusted their guarantees, but I decided to run anyway. I believed, if they later wanted me to leave, I could easily find another business or organization that would see the benefit of employing a state representative. As it turned out, I did not have to worry. I lost by 123 votes in a three-county primary.

Following my election defeat, in 1993, I returned to serve again as chairman of the party. In 1994, I helped candidates in the statewide elections, including for governor. Republicans took control of the House of Representatives for the first time in forty years. Later, I helped shore up home support for a presidential candidate.

During his campaign, I had taken the newly elected Republican governor around to all the local community leaders. As a reward, he invited me to his inauguration and asked me to the Governor's Mansion in Nashville. That next year, on a trip to the American Hospital Association annual meeting in Washington, D.C., my fellow delegates were curious to know how I had come to be on a first-name basis with all the Tennessee politicians with whom we met. These were the best of my political years, and Jim Whitlock was jealous, as I soon found out.

I gave my resume to this governor's administration for consideration for appointment to the Tennessee Health Facilities Commission. Since I worked in healthcare, I would serve as a representative of that industry. Officials gave my application to THA for their review, which was the normal process.

I was waiting to hear back when Jim Whitlock asked me to notarize his oath of office and appointment to the commission. He looked into my eyes and smiled wryly. Jim had used his higher status in THA to thwart my efforts and get himself selected. He never told me he had sent a competing application.

Over time, as the national Republican Party moved further and further to the right, I grew disillusioned. I had always been much more moderate than my political peers. I felt increasingly isolated within a party that had dramatically changed from the one I joined. This dissatisfaction led me eventually to leave the Republican Party.

CHAPTER
7

As Bradley Memorial Hospital moved into 1997, ominous financial, legal, and political clouds hung over it in a complicated tapestry of issues. Donna Hubbard continued her attacks on the hospital. She renewed efforts to gain community support for its sale by stoking fear that citizens were looking at a dramatic increase in their property taxes without this decision. Donna proclaimed the hospital to be in financial trouble, an assertion that the hospital board and Jim denied. She said it would be best to sell now to get the top price. Donna proposed a study commission to look at potential offers to recommend to the county commission and the public.

Public assurances notwithstanding, there were growing concerns within the hospital about its financial position. Month to month profits were diminishing, and it seemed that if nothing changed, we would soon see losses. The situation prompted Jim to call for a million-dollar cut in operational expenses by the end of the fiscal year, June 30, 1997. It would come from the hospital's hundred-million-dollar budget. He set up a task force to develop cost reduction measures.

This group focused on reducing job positions as a vital cost reduction goal. Establishing a flexible budget became a high priority too. A flexible budget is one that adjusts, or flexes, with changes in volume and activity. It is more sophisticated than the static budgets the hospital had always used. Fixed accounts remain the same from the time they are prepared and approved.

Jim knew his cost-reduction task force's success was critical to the hospital's phase three construction plans. He envisioned the initiative to be a fifteen- to eighteen-million-dollar project. The Board of Trustees had already given preliminary approval to this third construction phase, including reducing staff to help pay for it. The plan required eliminating one hundred full-time employees over five years. A reduction of the first twenty positions would occur in the new fiscal year beginning July 1, 1997. These twenty positions were in addition to the one-million-dollar cost savings envisioned by June 30.

The cost reduction task force's efforts ended in miserable failure, never coming close to achieving the one-million-dollar cost reduction goal. Committee members could not agree on anything, arguing that their departments and special projects should not suffer. Instead, they pointed fingers in other directions. They compensated by concentrating on the "low hanging fruit" on which everyone agreed. Such efforts allowed the committee to be active but produced little cost savings. None of the committee members understood flexible budgets or how to implement one. They spent considerable time, however, discussing and debating the topic. After reaching no consensus, another task force took up the issue.

In September 1997, Bradley Memorial recorded its first monthly loss in fifteen years, an alarming event. Jim staked his reputation on always producing a positive bottom line. In reflecting on the hundred-thousand-dollar loss for September (insignificant compared to those to come), Jim became emotional and cried at the senior management meeting. He demanded we concentrate on turning the hospital's finances around.

By October, Sam Bettis appointed a financial task force, directed by the board, to oversee efforts. When he announced the committee, Sam called for dramatic cuts. He named me secretary of the task force and asked that I keep detailed minutes. It replaced Jim's cost reduction group.

The collapse of Bradley Memorial's finances led to the scrapping of various plans to expand services, including its RediMed initiative. RediMed began in the emergency room as a "fast track" program. Designers envisioned providing quicker services for patients who presented to the emergency room with conditions requiring immediate care but not severe enough for full emergency services. The idea was to create an alternative treatment pathway that was faster than integrating them into the general emergency room patient population.

The intention was for RediMed to compete, inside the hospital, with the urgent or walk-in clinics cropping up in the community. The success within the emergency room led to its move to a nearby standalone clinic. I directed the change. Preparations, which I also oversaw, were underway to expand RediMed to other locations within the community when the hospital shut down the entire project, including the one clinic.

❖ ❖ ❖

At this time, Donna Hubbard also became involved in the hospital's legal matters. Opponents filed a lawsuit in early 1997, challenging the hospital's authority to engage in joint venture agreements. They alleged that Bradley Memorial Hospital, as a governmental entity, had no authority to engage in any joint venture or co-ownership agreements with private individuals or entities.

The plaintiff's attorney sought documents under Tennessee's open records statute. Encouraged by Donna, he attended the Board of Trustees and county commission meetings, asking questions. As a result, the *Cleveland Daily Banner* began reporting his actions and requesting information themselves.

The hospital's joint venture, Bradley Building, was at the center of the controversy. By then, Bradley Memorial's ownership interest in the business had become public, and it alarmed opponents. The plaintiffs alleged the arrangement was illegal under Article II, Section 29 of the Tennessee Constitution, which forbade all governments from engaging in private enterprises. The claimants asserted that because Bradley County owned the hospital, it was a governmental entity and subject to the state constitution.

In filing the lawsuit, the group's lawyer said, "The hospital is a child who has gone astray, and the court should discipline it."

In his public remarks, the opponent's attorney referenced the total assets of Bradley Memorial and how the hospital had acted without county commission approval. "The hospital board and administration have yanked a 140-million-dollar facility out to the hands of the public. The county commission needs to stop them immediately."

In response to this argument, the hospital attorney, Mike Callaway, asserted that the private act established Bradley Memorial as a quasi-governmental entity. It was, therefore, legally and solely directed by its Board of Trustees. The county's only control in the hospital's functions was in its ability to borrow money.

Donna joined in the public dispute, supporting the challengers and echoing the plaintiff attorney's assertions. She emphasized that, through its joint ventures, the hospital had benefited at the expense of private businesses. She said the Board of Trustees had "dropped the ball when it comes to looking out for the county's interests."

In recalling that the county commission had previously denied the project's approval, Donna asserted, "Whitlock, with the support of the hospital board, entered into an agreement forbidden by the

Bradley County Commission. They used an alias, Bradley Building, to go around this legislative body. In my opinion, we have an administrator at the hospital that does anything and everything he wants, regardless of what the county commission likes or dislikes. The board does whatever Whitlock requests. It's surprising how they ask so few questions at those board meetings."

Jim Whitlock countered Donna's comments. "Our Board of Trustees and management staff are disappointed in Donna Hubbard's attempt to manipulate the county commission and mislead the public in favor of her arguments. Most of them are without merit."

Mike Callaway also countered that the hospital was doing nothing that other hospitals in Tennessee were not also doing. He said it was standard operational practice.

The chancellor later ruled in favor of the plaintiffs. He refused to delay his order pending appeal to the Tennessee Court of Appeals. Soon after, the appeals court upheld the ruling. (Eventually, the Tennessee Supreme Court overturned the chancellor's and the court of appeals' decisions, but by then, the case had already inflicted severe damage on Bradley Memorial Hospital.)

The chancellor's decision had the immediate effect of shutting down every joint venture of Bradley Memorial, including the Ocoee Health Alliance (OHA). The hospital had started the OHA joint venture to bring together various healthcare providers, a preferred insurance company, and the hospital into a marketing strategy. The idea was to provide healthcare insurance to area businesses with the hospital as its sole provider. OHA was restructured and continued operating but without Bradley Memorial as a partner.

The hospital also had to restructure its agreement with the newly planned Cleveland Family YMCA. The revised agreement replaced what was originally to be a straightforward million-dollar joint venture agreement. It was a lease arrangement that included a provision for Bradley Memorial to build out its own space for a new physical therapy outpatient clinic.

Finally, the judge's decision crippled the hospital's new Health-Works deal. Little known to the public at the time, this initiative became the catalyst of the most significant controversy in Bradley Memorial Hospital's history. The hospital and a local physician group signed a declaration of intent on December 23, 1996.

HealthWorks of Cleveland, LLC, was to be an industrial occupational healthcare center supplying medical services to local industries, including comprehensive management of work-related injuries, mandated surveillance examinations, and aid in following OSHA, ADA, and FMLA guidelines. The hospital was to supply funding in the form of monthly loans until the establishment of the LLC. In exchange, Bradley Memorial would receive a fifty-percent ownership interest. Using the name HealthWorks of Tennessee, PC, the physician group was running a walk-in clinic. It would continue to do so under the joint agreement.

The HealthWorks joint venture was a disaster from the beginning. Initiated just as the hospital's other joint venture arrangements came under legal challenge, it was a failure from the start. The marketing effort to industry went poorly. Industrial leaders were apprehensive of the program due to the hospital's medical office building lawsuit.

From the outset, Bradley Memorial felt the financial burden of HealthWorks. Fighting and finger-pointing among the principals began. What started positively at the beginning of 1997, Jim declared dead in July. By August, Jim informed the senior managers that the solvency of HealthWorks was in question. Still, the hospital continued to make monthly payments supporting it, eventually paying a total of $564,000.

Bradley Memorial had nothing to show for its HealthWorks investment. Jim began seeking reimbursement from the physician partners, but they could not repay. Instead, they offered to sell their interest to the hospital for the loan amount. It was an untenable offer, as the hospital was under legal scrutiny for its medical office building project. Buying HealthWorks would expose the hospital's role in another joint venture, creating more public outcry.

With the hospital unwilling to buy HealthWorks, the physicians sold it to Columbia/HCA Healthcare Corporation, leaving Bradley Memorial no other choice but to sue for repayment later.

However, Jim Whitlock's and the board's most immediate concern after the court ruling was not HealthWorks but Bradley Building. The court decree required the hospital to divest its ownership interest in the company, forcing SunTrust to call its loan. The bank's action brought the project to an immediate halt. The hospital's two partners showed their willingness to let the loan default. They had no financial interest in the project. They had entered into the medical office building's development with no personal guaranty, no investment, and no risk of personal loss. As a result, the hospital board authorized Jim to negotiate with other potential buyers to take over the project in consultation with Hospital Attorney Mike Callaway.

Several frantic days followed, especially after Jim found out about Community Health System's plan. Their strategy was to buy the project when it went up for bid on the courthouse steps on December 4, 1997. CHS, a Nashville based hospital chain, had purchased Cleveland Community from HCA after Jim Whitlock came to work for Bradley Memorial. The hospital could not allow its competitor to control such a strategic asset.

In desperation, Jim negotiated a deal with Healthcare Realty Trust (HRT), a real estate investment trust from Nashville, Tennessee. They would buy the project before bidding began. Jim signed a contract binding Bradley Memorial to an upfront agreement to get their involvement. Bradley Memorial would fully lease the entire property, the building, and parking lot from the new owners.

The contract was not at all favorable to the hospital. HRT required nine hundred thousand dollars a year to lease the office space and thirty-eight thousand dollars per month to rent the parking lot.

The agreement allowed Bradley Memorial to sublease space to physicians. HRT promised to help fill up the building. Still, after one year following its completion, most of it was empty. Physician groups occupied only the fourth floor and half of the first.

Jim signed a twenty-year contract binding the hospital to lease the entire building as if it were full, and there was no incentive for HRT to help recruit. It was "shelled in" construction, meaning the interior space remained unfinished until the tenants signed a lease. After signing an agreement, HRT then had to pay a specific fixed build-out cost for the leased space. It was more beneficial to HRT for the medical office building to be unoccupied. If there were no tenants, the build-out money went unspent.

Once HRT completed and turned the building over, it immediately drained the hospital's finances.

The leases for this new medical office building were also expensive for physicians, complicating recruitment efforts. Doctors found it cheaper to lease or build elsewhere. In an anxious attempt to recruit Cleveland's Internal Medicine Group (IMG) to be the first tenants, Jim, with board approval, fully leased their old medical facility located nearby with no immediate plans to occupy it. By this means, IMG became the new building's first occupants, taking up the entire fourth floor. The arrangement with IMG also left the hospital with a substantial financial liability since it had to begin making payments on their former offices.

❖ ❖ ❖

Taking advantage of the court ruling against the hospital in Bradley Building, Jim Whitlock again renewed efforts to find a buyer. Barring such a sale, he proposed a complete restructuring of Bradley Memorial Hospital, turning over the hospital assets and operation to a community-based 501(c) (3) nonprofit organization.

Both paths were problematic. It had been less than a year since the hospital had beaten back the Erlanger Health System proposal. Bill Ledford and most other county commissioners still opposed such a sale. Also, Bill was adamantly against the idea of turning Bradley Memorial into a 501(c) (3). He said Bradley County would never give up ownership of the hospital, even to a local organization. Bill said he would kill it regardless of Jim's wishes.

Still, Jim moved ahead on both fronts. He met with Columbia/ HCA Healthcare Corporation, Tenet Healthcare Corporation, and other for-profit healthcare company officials. Jim's meeting with Community Health Systems, however, was the most serious. He flew to the company's headquarters in Nashville to discuss a potential sale with corporate officials. Jim presented his findings to the Board of Trustees, who were unmoved in their opposition. They were more receptive to restructuring the hospital into a 501(c) (3). But, after efforts to persuade Bill Ledford failed, they dropped that idea too. There was no clear path forward as the hospital descended into further financial distress.

❖ ❖ ❖

The upcoming 1998 local elections also played a significant role in these proceedings. Gary Davis was actively developing plans throughout 1997 to run for county executive for a second time. He believed he would be challenging Donna Hubbard, who would be running for a fourth term. I was fully supportive of Gary's effort, spending a great deal of time in an unofficial role as a campaign advisor. I could concentrate on Gary's election because my term as Republican Party Chairman had ended in March 1997. Being term-limited, I was glad to give up the party's reins and spend my efforts on other matters. I had spent most of the decade in the role.

Gary's political plans brought the wrath of Donna Hubbard. She used the hospital's legal and financial problems against him. Along with the other joint venture deals, Donna notably tied Gary to the failed HealthWorks effort. By then, it had become a major public issue despite Jim's best efforts to keep it quiet.

Donna also announced she was not running for reelection. Instead, she would throw her support behind Carl Shrewsbury, her longtime executive assistant. Donna then spent the rest of the campaign attacking Gary, associating him with all the alleged failures of Jim Whitlock and Bradley Memorial Hospital.

As 1998 began, the financial, legal, and political uncertainty that had plagued Bradley Memorial Hospital throughout 1997 only intensified.

CHAPTER
8

January 1998 began in a total financial panic. Behind the scenes and out of sight from most of the hospital staff and the public, Jim and the board were melting down. The fear was toothsome, and they were panic-stricken. After deciding that neither a sale of the hospital nor converting it to at 501(c) (3) nonprofit organization were practical options, the Board of Trustees began demanding a concerted effort to cut costs. They mainly focused on layoffs as the primary means to achieve this goal. Bob Sain chaired the Financial Task Force set up by Board Chairman Sam Bettis, and he emphasized the need for action.

However, Jim had not given up on selling the hospital, and he brought another offer to the board for their consideration. CHS's second offer was a joint ownership arrangement. They would give Bradley County a forty-nine percent ownership interest in Bradley Memorial, while CHS would own fifty-one percent. The Board of Trustees at once dismissed the offer because majority ownership meant control of the hospital would pass to CHS.

Cash flow issues developed in March. Craig Taylor announced the hospital could not make its annual bond payment of $1.4 million. Jim Whitlock exploded in rage. Craig averted the crisis only because he obtained a million-dollar credit line with Cleveland Bank & Trust to relieve the immediate concern.

Shortly afterward, Jim and some members of the board pressured Craig to resign. Sensing his tenuous situation, Craig began applying for other jobs. Sam Bettis and Bob Sain, who were still supportive, resisted Jim's push. They saved Craig for the moment.

The hospital's financial status continued to deteriorate. By July 1, 1998, the beginning of the new fiscal year, Jim and the board called for a contingency plan to reduce the budget by ten percent, if necessary. By September, Craig projected a loss for the fiscal year ending June 30, 1999, at more than two million dollars. No one knew what to do.

The Financial Task Force bogged down, as the crisis paralyzed Bob Sain. He was clueless when it came to hospital finances. Senior managers were at each other's throats, unable to agree on the most elemental of changes. I became the focus of their hostility as I increasingly challenged their groupthink mentality.

The senior managers' immediate ire centered on my efforts to reorganize the emergency room into a single cohesive department. The idea was to integrate the registration function and patient care under one director. Jim called the concept a "super department" and assigned me to organize it. The intent was to streamline the entire system to improve efficiency and shorten wait times for emergency room patients.

The effort proved difficult. I clashed with the nursing director, who took exception to the emergency room nurse manager reporting to anyone but her. I collided with Craig Taylor over how the integration would affect registration under the new structure. My opponents set about to kill the concept by both overt and covert means. They enlisted the help of others on the senior management team. Since I had no friends within the group, everyone focused on me. Their attacks became increasingly personal and vicious.

The director of the Bradley Healthcare Foundation, a member

of the senior management team, sensed the financial disaster that lay ahead and resigned to work for one of the consultants that advised the foundation. Jim named Dewayne Belew the new director, who would also continue in his role as Director of Marketing and Public Relations.

❖ ❖ ❖

Jim Whitlock was absent through much of this time. He took frequent trips to the Medical University of South Carolina in Charleston to pursue a doctorate in healthcare management. Bradley Memorial paid for the entire cost of the program. Jim had started in 1997 and was well on his way to completing the degree by the time Bradley Memorial's fiscal crisis became acute. During this time of financial peril, Jim saw an advantage for himself. Jim's dissertation topic would dictate the hospital's response.

Jim announced to the senior managers that he was starting a process to reengineer the entire hospital, and the plan would include them. Reengineering refers to a systematic starting over and reinventing the way a company gets its work done.

The timeframe indicated that the process would happen over the next several months. It would consist of steps to stabilize the hospital's finances. By the end, Jim predicted that not everyone would be in their same roles.

Jim announced the choice of two distinct groups to achieve this goal. First, Jim named his friend, David Zimmerman, and his company, Zimmerman & Associates, as consultants, to review the hospital's finances. They would recommend changes and offer alternatives for restructuring the hospital's internal operations. Zimmerman & Associates would place its emphasis on the business office and the senior management team. Jim also hired two University of Tennessee professors to serve as executive coaches.

In many ways, these two selections were at cross purposes, as their reengineering approaches were vastly different. Reengineering consultants look primarily at the organization's processes. They recommend changes based on industry standards, emphasizing cutting across organizational and functional boundaries to produce results. These consultants rely on empirical data using leading benchmark and best practices databases to make these recommendations.

Executive coaching is a professional relationship between a trained coach and an individual or group. Through a process of examination, discourse, and the use of specific tools, the coach serves as a resource. It is the executive coach's goal to help the group or individual examine and develop their decision-making. They lead the group or individual to experiment with new ways of thinking or interacting. They also commit the group or individual to pledge to action steps that help achieve their goals.

Through this method, the organization's leader or leaders create the reengineered organization. Executive coaches often study leaders using testing instruments such as 360-degree feedback, the Myers-Briggs Type Indicator® (MBTI®), and the Strength Deployment Inventory® (SDI®).

An executive coach uses the 360-degree feedback technique to gather responses. The feedback includes information about a leader's strengths and development needs, how others perceive them, and what they need to do to achieve a higher performance level and positive impact. The list of feedback providers usually includes anyone who has enough familiarity with the leader's work to contribute useful observations and suggestions. Feedback participants typically include all direct reports, managers, and peers. Through this feedback loop, the leader gains insight into their perceived effectiveness and enhances their self-awareness and ability to make decisions objectively.

MBTI® is an assessment tool developed using Swiss psychiatrist

Carl Jung's analysis of human behavior. In his research, Jung saw that humans are born with particular preferences for using their minds in diverse ways. Jung believed that although all individuals can process information, there are natural, inborn differences in how they do it. These differences determine how we make decisions. Understanding these natural penchants improves our understanding of the decision-making process, not only in ourselves but also in others. The MBTI® tool helps people discover their preferences. This new awareness fosters improved decision making.

SDI® is an instrument that helps a person find their strengths in dealing with others under two conditions: when things are going well, and when they face conflict. A graph highlights the results from data that comes from the answers of the individual's self-survey. The chart shows the person's motivational value system and conflict sequence.

For his dissertation, Jim was interested in studying both approaches (reengineering consultants and executive coaches) in the hospital's restructuring process. Specifically, he wanted to learn the effect that leadership style had on reengineering success or failure. Jim hypothesized that the method employed (i.e., an executive coach versus a reengineering consultant) impacted the outcome. He specifically said he wanted to use 360-degree feedback, the Myers-Briggs Type Indicator®, and the Strength Deployment Inventory® in his analysis. As a result, over the next year, Bradley Memorial Hospital became Jim Whitlock's real-life research project.

❖ ❖ ❖

As 1998 progressed, HealthWorks became the predominant public issue. While Donna Hubbard was not running for reelection, she remained focused on the race to succeed her. Donna hoped her efforts to expose the hospital would help Carl Shrewsbury defeat Gary Davis.

Donna continued to team up with the attorney who'd brought suit against Bradley Memorial over its joint ventures, asserting the Health-Works deal was an illegal scheme concocted by Jim Whitlock to award physicians. Not only had the Board of Trustees failed to approve the joint venture, but they also argued Jim had exceeded the spending ceiling set without board approval.

Nervously, Jim asked me to research the board minutes to find references to HealthWorks discussion or approval. I found three separate board meetings (October 1996, February 1997, and May 1997), where board members discussed the project. Jim never asked for approval, and the board never gave it.

Jim was aware there was a ten-thousand-dollar spending limit. At his request, I had previously researched the board minutes to find the policy. Jim told me he would expend funds regardless of what the minutes said, as long as he had money in the budget.

Donna called for an independent audit of Bradley Memorial Hospital. Jim and Craig appeared before the county commission to answer questions. Following their presentation, the county commission voted against funding the proposed audit. Chairman Bill Ledford once again quashed Donna's effort.

After the county commission meeting, Sam Bettis formed an ad hoc committee of the Board of Trustees to review the hospital's current expenditure policies. The goal was to develop a new limit on what the administrator could authorize without board approval. Sam appointed me to the committee and wanted to know if the board had ever adopted such a policy and what the amount was. For this second review, I expanded my research.

Former Administrator Bill Torrence recalled the limit was once ten thousand dollars, but later it increased to twenty-five thousand dollars. I was aware of the resolution passed in August 1984, authorizing ten thousand dollars. It was increased from the previous spending limit of five thousand dollars. After Bill's recollection, I researched further but could not find where the board had ever increased it again.

The policy was outdated. By 1998, it was almost impossible to make a hospital purchase that did not exceed ten thousand dollars. Still, that was the official policy. Both $10,000 and $25,000, nevertheless, are less than the HealthWorks payments of $564,000. I believed Donna Hubbard might have a legitimate argument that the payout to HealthWorks was illegal.

❖ ❖ ❖

The public debate over HealthWorks continued as the election for Bradley County Executive heated up. The Republican primary featured three candidates: Gary Davis; Carl Shrewsbury; and David Gilbert.

For Gary, Donna's announcement she was not running for reelection was fortuitous. He had expected a tight race. Now the only thing standing in his way was the primary. However, Gary was upset to discover that Donna's executive assistant, Carl Shrewsbury, was to run as a Republican and not a Democrat. Gary would now have a formidable primary opponent.

Carl explained he had always been a Republican, his primary voting record attesting to the fact, despite working for Donna Hubbard. He assembled a strong campaign team and had Donna's full backing.

David Gilbert was a businessman who self-funded his campaign. Politically active in many earlier campaigns as a fundraiser, he was now stepping out to run for political office himself. He had supporters who controlled much of the party's finances. David also took control of the party apparatus by helping his son get elected Chairman of the Bradley County Republican Party when I stepped down.

In his campaign, Carl Shrewsbury said he would stand for the hospital employees' interests if chosen. But he also mirrored Donna's opposition and questioned Gary's role in its financial and legal woes. He specifically targeted HealthWorks, asking what role Gary had played.

Gary disavowed having any part in the deal, saying it never had board approval. I knew Gary's denial was only partially true. After joining the Board of Trustees, Gary had spent most of his time, like the other trustees, rubberstamping all Sam Bettis and Jim Whitlock's initiatives. I had to help Gary recall the issue. From my conversations with him, it was clear Gary remembered little about the project.

Gary feared David Gilbert's campaign would siphon votes away from him, a fear that was well-founded. David's campaign had the appearance of success. He blanked the local news media with ads and placed hundreds, if not thousands, of yard signs throughout the county.

However, Gary concentrated his attention on Carl Shrewsbury, believing his campaign was most detrimental to his.

Recognizing hospital employees and their families were an influential voting bloc, under the Tennessee Open Records Act, Gary obtained a complete mailing list of hospital personnel. I helped him compose the direct mail piece attacking Carl Shrewsbury and Donna Hubbard for their attempts to sell Bradley Memorial Hospital.

Cleveland Community Hospital's parent company also inadvertently assisted Gary's campaign. At the height of Community Health System's attempt to buy or jointly own Bradley Memorial, in their effort to show community support, they published an ad in the *Cleveland Daily Banner* listing all the members on Cleveland Community Hospital's board. The one member that got my attention was Carl Shrewsbury.

I prepared an attack ad that ran in the local newspaper questioning how Carl, as a member of the Board of Directors of Cleveland Community Hospital, could fairly represent Bradley Memorial. It accused him of an outlandish and outrageous conflict of interest. Afterward, stacks of this ad appeared at the employee timeclocks.

On the night of the May 5 primary, Gary Davis won by a narrow fifty-three votes over Carl Shrewsbury. David Gilbert came in a distant third. Gary went on to win the general election on August 6 against the Democrat by sixty-three percent of the vote.

We had hoped Gary's election would end Donna's attacks at the hospital, but that was not to be, at least not at once. Donna had decided to run for the state senate seat held by Jeff Miller, a Republican. Her decision meant the public debate about the hospital would continue for a few more months.

I met with Jeff to discuss strategy and tell him how to get the hospital's employee mailing list. Later, he campaigned in the employee parking lot and shook hands with staff members. In November, Jeff easily defeated Donna.

During Jeff's reelection campaign, he told me Donna Hubbard had met with District Attorney General Jerry Estes. The purpose was to start a criminal complaint against Jim Whitlock and the HealthWorks partners. I was alarmed but not surprised. It explained why Jim and Sam had shown so much interest in the hospital's spending policy. Jeff was a credible source. He was not sure where the investigation would lead, but Jeff thought I should know. He asked me not to tell anyone about the inquiry. I agreed to keep silent, but my mind gyrated as to where it would lead.

❖ ❖ ❖

In 1998, the hospital's significant visible issues centered on its finances, HealthWorks, and Gary's contest against Carl Shrewsbury. But there was another lesser-known, equally critical issue. Bradley Memorial's compliance matters began to come into focus.

On January 13, 1998, a subpoena arrived from the Department of Health and Human Services, Office of Inspector General, for pneumonia records. As the hospital's risk manager, I received the subpoena and sent a copy to Mike Callaway. In a panic, Jim discussed the subpoena with Mike but, against my advice, decided not to inform the trustees. He also did not review it with the other senior managers.

On June 16, 1998, Compliance Concepts, Inc., hired by the hospital to review its billing procedures, presented a long-anticipated risk assessment to the senior managers about hospital compliance issues they had found. It was an eye-opening report that included details of the pneumonia case. After the presentation, Jim took up all the copies. He told us these issues were to be kept quiet due to the information's sensitivity and the political climate. The report remained buried for months.

❖ ❖ ❖

On August 13, 1998, a team from the Department of Justice and the FBI arrived at the hospital. Their purpose was to interview the Director of Medical Records and other employees in that department, Craig Taylor, and Jim Whitlock about pneumonia upcoding. I was not alerted to their arrival and would not have known but for a news media inquiry. Someone had alerted the *Cleveland Daily Banner* to the presence of federal law enforcement officials. After the reporter's question, Jim informed the senior managers that Justice Department personnel and the FBI were there. He and Dewayne Belew had issued a press release.

The article that appeared in the newspaper on August 14 was misleading. It was a deliberate fabrication to portray the event as routine—a review to assess the hospital's compliance plan. This plan did not even exist at that time. After the investigators left, I again encouraged Jim to report the pneumonia upcoding case to the Board of Trustees, but he said no. An entire year passed before he did.

❖ ❖ ❖

As 1998 ended, I debated whether I should stay at Bradley Memorial Hospital. The environment was toxic. The other senior executives had singled me out and attacked as each envisioned an uncertain future for themselves. Based on my unhealthy relationships with Jim and the other senior managers, I knew I was in jeopardy. However, I decided to stay because my work was still significant. I concluded I had no control over Jim Whitlock, the other senior administrators, or the Board of Trustees and their decisions. I could only affect my areas of responsibility. I felt a duty to stay, watch out for the departments under my control, and ensure the best hospital care possible for our patients. I had an obligation to the community to watch out for their interests, know what was happening, and supply a voice of reason as things began to fall apart. With these issues haunting it, Bradley Memorial Hospital entered 1999.

CHAPTER
9

By 1999, the composition of the Board of Trustees had changed. Sam Bettis, Bob Cantrell, and Bob Sain were still serving. Joining them over the past decade were four new members: Eddie Duncan, M.D.; Don Lorton; Lou Pattern; and Bobbie Atchley.

Though Sam Bettis and Jim Whitlock continued to dominate the Board of Trustees, new members Don Lorton and Lou Patten brought a freshness to the group as they began asking more thoughtful and probing questions. After their appointments, I was optimistic their additions would bring needed change. But, even with their more challenging approach, both deferred to Sam's and Jim's leadership. The board continued to be a fairly reliable rubber stamp.

The new year saw a continuing decline in Bradley Memorial's finances. The findings of hospital auditors compounded these month-to-month losses. The hospital would have to make a $2.2 million pension adjustment in its upcoming audited financial statements. That amount, along with a $750,000 operating loss, meant a total loss for the 1997 to 1998 fiscal year of three million dollars. Additionally, Bradley Memorial began making monthly lease payments to HRT, which placed the hospital at once into cashflow problems for the 1998 to 1999 fiscal year.

The hospital had to secure another million-dollar line of credit to help. Later, it defaulted on an AmSouth Bank loan of $2.8 million. In response to these financial developments, Jim said, "I have a year to turn things around."

With these turns of events, Jim renewed his efforts to force Craig's resignation. Sam Bettis's and Bob Sain's opposition had thwarted his attempt, but this time he was successful.

Jim, Sam, Gary Davis, and I were on the annual trip to the American Hospital Association's meeting in Washington, D.C., when the resignation finally came. I had taken the AHA trip in late January or early February every year for about a decade with Jim and Sam. Gary began attending after his appointment to the hospital board. He decided to go in 1999 even though he had resigned from the board. We intended to hear about federal legislation affecting hospitals, meet with the Tennessee congressional delegation, and lobby in support or opposition to current bills.

While we were there, Jim took the opportunity to urge Gary to support his push for Craig's resignation. During the AHA meeting, Jim, Sam, and Bob debated the issue back and forth. Bob was in Cleveland but joined the discussion by telephone. Sam and Bob gave in only after Jim gave them an ultimatum—it would be either Craig's resignation or his, and they could decide. As a result, on February 2, while we were still at the AHA meeting, Craig called Jim to say he had written and given his resignation. He gave a month's notice.

When Jim gave me the news, I tried to act surprised. He must have been able to tell I was faking, because he said, "Now Michael, I'm sure you knew all about it."

I did not reply, diverting the subject and asking what the hospital would do for a CFO in the interim.

After returning from the trip, Jim announced at a department head meeting that Craig was leaving for personal reasons. He also said Erlanger's former CFO, Ken Conner, would serve as Bradley Memorial's interim CFO. Jim eventually hired Ken Jackson, another noticeably young and inexperienced certified public accountant, to be the hospital's new CFO. He began work on June 1.

Jim also embarked on yet another effort to cut costs. This initiative took on much more urgency. Ken Conner had determined a $4.8 million adjustment would be necessary for the fiscal year ending on June 30. Jim promptly demanded a ten percent reduction in expenses, which threw senior management into immediate panic and continued disfunction.

Bradley Memorial's financial position was so alarming, members of the Bradley Healthcare Foundation met with the Board of Trustees. They suspended all fundraising efforts until the hospital's fiscal outlook improved. In response, Jim and the senior managers eventually produced a layoff plan.

Again, Jim mentioned the sale of Bradley Memorial Hospital as a practical possibility, eyeing either CHS or Erlanger as potential partners. If a deal were not possible, he would recommend a management agreement.

In response, Bill Ledford said, "The county commission will not go for it. If Bradley Memorial needs money, I can push through some financing until the hospital gets back on its feet."

Bill's offer was a risky but workable possibility that Jim never pursued, which was baffling to me. For his reasons, I concluded Jim preferred a sale, and securing funding from the county would thwart his goal.

After Craig Taylor's resignation, Jim never let a meeting pass without blaming him for all the hospital's financial ills. Whether it was a senior management meeting, board meeting, physician meeting, or another event, Jim was withering in his criticism of Craig.

Jim also looked to discredit Craig in our senior management meetings. Jim announced that Ken Conner had discovered thousands of dollars of checks in a desk drawer. Craig had cut the payments for vendors but never mailed them. It was an outrageous finding, but all of us knew Jim had been aware of the scheme. Craig had never decided anything without first consulting Jim.

In January 1999, Steve Bivens resigned as Chairman of the Bradley Healthcare Foundation. The wife of a prominent physician replaced him. Steve's choice to lead this fundraising group had been clear. His community status had given the foundation, whose sole beneficiary was Bradley Memorial Hospital, immediate credibility. Steve, a former state representative, had great insight into and knowledge of both the political and business community of Cleveland and Bradley County. He'd been the perfect choice. Steve's resignation was significant. It signaled growing unease within the county, not only about the hospital's financial status but also about rumors of its legal troubles.

By that time, speculation had been swirling within the community about some ongoing investigations. No one exactly knew what was happening. These rumors reached fever pitch after the FBI raided Woods Memorial Hospital in nearby Etowah in February. Reports also circulated that local doctors were testifying before the Bradley County Grand Jury. One doctor said he was in the clear but had implicated others.

Reports were out that HealthWorks was under investigation. The FBI was going to raid Bradley Memorial Hospital just as they had Woods Memorial. Rumors of a pneumonia billing fraud investigation at Bradley Memorial were also circulating. Speculated dollar amounts ranged anywhere from one million to ten million. Bradley Memorial's coding frequency for pneumonia was one of the highest in the nation.

I never confirmed or denied the rumors about the pneumonia issue or any other investigation for anyone who asked. I only conceded that there were many rumors about various matters. However, I had inside knowledge about the pneumonia inquiry. I was also mindful of what the state senator had told me in late 1998 about the local investigation.

There was also a federal grand jury investigation involving Bradley Memorial and Jim Whitlock underway in neighboring Chattanooga. The grand jury there was looking at the pneumonia case, which was a civil matter but had criminal elements. I thought it might also involve other unlawful issues. Jim had hired a prominent Chattanooga criminal defense attorney to be his legal representative in those proceedings. Information coming out of the federal grand jury was impossible to obtain. I remained watchful of both the state and federal probes.

In this environment, Jim called me into his office after we returned from the AHA meeting in Washington, D.C. He told me I would be taking over the hospital's compliance initiatives, which had previously been the responsibility of Craig Taylor. He asked me to put together a compliance timeline, plotting the steps forward with a deadline for sending a final plan for approval to the Board of Trustees by September.

Jim also directed me to assume responsibility for every hospital contract and centralize the process. Up to that time, the hospital had used a fragmented, decentralized contract negotiation method. At the next senior management meeting, Jim directed everyone to turn over to me all original professional or service contracts senior managers had in their possession.

My new role did not sit well with them. Larry Ingram, the senior manager responsible for medical staff credentialing, refused to hand over the physician contracts.

Larry was jealous and petty. He displayed every symptom of Short Man's Syndrome, a trait he shared with Jim. It was difficult for him to watch as others were given greater responsibilities or received accolades. Larry harbored every slight, even Jim Whitlock's. If Larry could pay you back, he did. My standoff with him over physician contracts continued until I left Bradley Memorial.

I was suspicious of Jim's motives. It would now be easy for him to blame me as the compliance officer for the pneumonia case or any other billing issue. If I handled all contracts, it would be easy to point the finger at me if an agreement, such as the Ramsey Group contract, was determined to be illegal.

In going through Craig's compliance files, I found the Compliance Concepts, Inc. report. It was the findings presented to senior management on June 16, 1998. Jim had taken up all the copies afterward. Craig had simply filed them away with little or no action taken to address the many issues. I used this report extensively as I moved ahead to develop a compliance plan.

❖ ❖ ❖

In June, the Tennessee Hospital Association selected Jim Whitlock as the recipient of the Meritorious Service Award for CEO. They would announce it publicly in the fall. It was ironic given the severe financial and legal matters underway at the hospital where he was the CEO. But even as these matters were swirling around him, Jim took comfort in THA's recognition and moved ahead to restructure the hospital.

❖ ❖ ❖

Through much of early 1999, Jim focused on this organizational reform initiative. By the middle of the year, he was ready to implement it. Because I knew Jim's ulterior motive was his dissertation, I had a jaundiced view. And I did not believe the outcome would be positive for me. I based my opinion on a conviction Jim expressed at the outset of the reengineering process: "I don't view you as a team player."

The two University of Tennessee professors divided up the executive coaching initiative, each taking on defined roles. One would work with all the senior managers, while the other would focus on a select group of middle managers.

In our first group meeting in January, one of them said, "Your organization is top-heavy." It was a precise observation given that senior management at that time consisted of eight members, including Jim. His statement also acknowledged the direction his review would take. Over the next several months, each senior manager met with him many times individually.

We completed the Myers-Briggs Type Indicator® skill assessment inventory and the Strength Deployment Inventory®, both of which were supposed to be confidential.

My personality type using MBTI® was INTJ, one of the rarest types in the human population. Sometimes referred to as "the mastermind," INTJs are introverted individuals who focus on ideas and concepts rather than facts and details. They make decisions based on logic and reason and prefer planning and organization over spontaneity and flexibility. INTJs are typically intellectual, independent, and selective about their relationships, choosing to associate with those who are intellectually stimulating. No wonder I did not fit in with Jim Whitlock's chaotic, disorganized senior management team.

My SDI® score showed I was a blend of two behavior types: analytic-autonomizing and assertive-directing. My conduct did not change with the circumstances. In other words, I would give the same response when things were going well or when faced with conflict. Analytic-autonomizing people are thinkers, planners, and analyzers, while assertive-directing people are winners, go-getters, and fighters. The blend of these two is judicious-competing. This blend seeks gratification by employing strategies in dealing with others wherein one uses their head to win. They want to outwit their opponents within the limits of the rules. My SDI® score was an accurate description of my approach with my fellow senior managers and how I conducted myself during the crisis that lay ahead.

Every senior manager took part in 360-degree feedback. These appraisals were intended to supply anonymous and confidential feedback about a given person from people around them based on their myriad answers to a series of questions. In my case, I got feedback from Jim, senior managers, and direct reports. In theory, the interviewees are supposed to be anonymous. Still, it was easy to figure out who was giving what feedback upon review. I got negative reviews from Jim and the senior managers while earning high marks from my direct reports. Though all the assessments were supposed to be confidential, I never trusted that the information was not making its way back to Jim. After all, he had a dissertation to complete.

After the completion of all these leadership tests, I had a one-on-one session with one of the professors. At the conclusion, he said, "You're not in step with most of the others," which was not a surprise. After that, I had several coaching sessions with the professor. He asked me to think of ways I could integrate my skills with that of the others. I concluded it was a difficult challenge.

The other professor took charge of the middle manager executive coaching project. Jim asked each senior manager to nominate subordinate managers who reported directly to them as candidates to take part in the task force. Because Jim was to make the final selections, I saw this step as useless. He would set up the committee as he wished. Still, I took part and nominated several of my managers. In the end, Jim chose some of them.

The formation of the task force became a contention source among many middle managers. Those not selected expressed their disappointment and wondered what they had done to merit exclusion. Suspicions arose after the professor announced the group would meet in quasi secrecy and had to pledge silence. The information shared was not to leave the room. They held meetings in the new external physical plant facility, far away from the other hospital meeting rooms. Adding to the mystery element, the members traveled through the hospital's new underground connecting tunnel to get there.

The group's purpose was to develop a reengineered hospital from top to bottom. There were no forbidden concepts. The task force could freely debate each element or proposal.

The group took to their new role with zest. Jim became alarmed by the speed of their deliberations and looked to slow them down. He began attending some of the meetings, which had the desired effect of "putting the brakes on," as he called it. Jim had Sam Bettis appoint board member Don Lorton to the group, which further slowed the group's progress. It was clear that Jim wanted their conclusions to fit into his timeline.

I did not ask for the information, but since I had several loyalists within the task force's ranks, they updated me. I gathered from these reports that some members used their participation to protect their department. In contrast, others used it as an opportunity to advance their careers. It was with this backdrop that the task force released its final report after months of meetings. Their recommendations were more of a lackluster textbook approach.

While the two University of Tennessee professors promoted executive coaching as a reengineering method, Zimmerman & Associates moved forward with a more traditional approach. They first developed a plan to reengineer the hospital's business operations, calling it the Department of Patient Financial Services. They recommended a new director to oversee this expansive division. Again, Jim threw up an obstacle. He agreed to the concept, but instead of hiring a director at once, he delayed the decision.

The Zimmerman recommendations on senior management restructuring leaked before the top executives had seen them. The report called for a new structure to include a CEO, CFO, COO, CIO, and chief medical officer. Jim was unhappy with the proposal's premature release, but he nonetheless accepted it.

In May, Jim announced that dramatic changes for the hospital administration were coming by July. He would select a new, smaller senior management team. Jim promised we would all have jobs within the revised structure, but not necessarily the duties we currently held. Jim further directed that each senior manager draw up and present to him their organizational suggestions. He would consider these, along with those proposed from the reengineering efforts. My organizational chart mirrored Zimmerman's.

The coming changes created a great deal of chaos and fear within the current senior management group, with each member vying to remain in the top tier. I knew my exclusion from this new executive management structure was probable. I based my belief on my executive coaching sessions and my poor relationship with Jim. I would not go, however, without making a case to stay.

Jim asked me to personally sell Gary Davis and Bill Ledford on the restructuring effort, something I did not do. I thought, *Are you kidding me?* However, Jim did not wait for me. Shortly after asking, he discussed the changes with Gary and Bill. He told them I had nothing to fear. Regardless of the outcome, I would still have a job.

Both seemed comfortable with Jim's reassurance, even as I protested that if Jim demoted me, I could not survive. As a subordinate, I could not compete with any of Jim's new team on an equal footing. I was being set up to fail. In separate meetings, Gary and Bill listened to my argument, but I made no headway, as neither intervened on my behalf. Both were more concerned about the hospital's looming fiscal crisis. They also did not understand the peril a demotion would have for my future at Bradley Memorial. I was disappointed in both of them.

Jim also announced there was to be a hospital-wide layoff by June.

Each of the senior managers had to draw up lists of positions from their departments for elimination. Over the next two months, aside from jockeying to stay atop the soon-to-be reengineered organization, senior management also grappled with this impending layoff. The fighting was intense as each person tried to protect their departments at the expense of others. A consensus was eventually reached that the largest department, nursing, should have the fewest cuts. This decision left the second-largest area, ancillary and service departments, which I oversaw, as the natural place to draw. The senior management group seemed to revel in making these cuts.

Some of the senior managers held a secret meeting. The topic of discussion was me. As told to me by a trusted confidant, the group discussed the need to include someone from hospital administration in the layoff. The assemblage quickly focused on me as the ideal candidate. They had not invited me to the meeting because I was the target of the organizers. These senior managers first agreed the entire group would approach Jim with the recommendation. But as they continued the discussion, they decided that only one should meet with him and speak for the whole group.

Faced with this knowledge, I was not sure what to do next. Jim had already assured everyone in senior management they would have jobs. How would he handle their recommendation? I believed my layoff would speed up his plan to use me as a scapegoat for all the compliance and billing issues that were certain to come. I imagined he would "discover" my misdeeds after I was gone.

By June, the layoff plan was in place. Jim presented it to the Board of Trustees at their annual retreat. It was a modest event, held nearby at the Whitewater Center along the Ocoee River in Polk County. The board held the meeting there to avoid the criticism of the more lavish events held in prior years.

Lou Patten and I rode to the retreat together. On the way, as we discussed the hospital's continuing financial troubles, Lou voiced his concerns about the impending layoffs and in Jim's continued leadership of the hospital.

"Jim can't survive," Lou said. "I'm working on a plan to present to the board to get his resignation."

I encouraged him. It was good news to know that a board member was finally willing to blame those responsible.

At the retreat, Jim introduced the plan to restructure senior management without naming any individuals to the new lineup. Jim asked the administrative team to leave the meeting before its presentation since he did not want any of us to know what positions were being eliminated and what new positions he was proposing. All of us left nervously, and apparently it met with the board's approval since it was soon implemented.

After the board retreat, the regular business of the hospital continued. Feeling confident about my bleak future, Doug Renz, the chief information officer and a member of senior management, decided to use a mundane issue to provoke me. I was not surprised Doug would do such a thing. I was, however, surprised at the vileness of the attack.

Doug, a late addition to the senior management team, was arrogant, snobbish, and ambitious. Doug believed he was the smartest senior team member and would do anything to climb over everyone else. Since every senior manager used information technology, Doug could interfere in everyone's work. He believed that by acting in grossly obsequious ways toward Jim, he could advance to the top.

I had negotiated a contract with a new physician to provide pathology services for the hospital. The hospital's pathologist was retiring, causing us to hire a new one. We finally reached an agreement, and I took the contract to Jim for his signature. One stipulation of the deal required the hospital to build a data interface between the pathology and the hospital systems at our expense. The arrangement would allow for the smooth transfer of data between the two entities. I took this part of the agreement to Doug, as the CIO, to execute. I saw it as a routine business transaction that the hospital needed to complete to get the new pathology services running.

Doug exploded in rage. "Why didn't you bring this agreement to me before signing it? I should have been in the negotiations. This interface will be expensive to build. Who's going to pay for it?"

"We're going to pay for the interface, Doug," I replied. "The hospital."

"And how did this get decided without my input? Who authorized it?"

"Jim did. He signed the contract."

"Well, you've fucked up, Michael. What you did is stupid, and if you don't acknowledge that you screwed up, you're stupid."

I had to act undisturbed. I knew Doug was trying to provoke me, hoping I would respond inappropriately. I had to restrain myself as I listened to Doug's obnoxious taunt.

"Listen," I said calmly. "Just build the interface. That's the only part you're responsible for. Your comments are inappropriate, Doug."

I walked out of his office, trembling with anger. It was the closest I had come to hitting someone since high school.

Growing up as a Baptist preacher's kid had made me tough. My dad moved the family often, going from one church pastorate to another. As a result, I was never anchored to any community, a crucial element to acceptance in the mountains of western North Carolina. Each place we moved provided challenges. I wasn't a bully, but neither would I be bullied. It was this attitude that led to fighting, most often at school but also at church and other places. It was always my initial instinct.

With Doug, however, in a split second, I had decided not to strike. I recognized it was what he wanted. In my mind, I could hear Doug telling Jim he had no idea why I had gotten violent, that I must be losing my mind.

I went to my office, closed the door, and sat there seething. It did not take long for Doug to apologize, but he did not have the integrity to do it in person.

He sent me an email that said, "I apologize for my poor choice of words."

I replied, "I acknowledge and accept your apology."

I didn't want to accept his apology, but it would be better to do nothing about the situation. If I took the matter to Jim, I would only invite an accusation against me. It was better to take the blow. I did not need to deal with another issue.

❖ ❖ ❖

A few days later, as the hospital progressed toward the layoff, I got a call at home from Lou.

"I had a conversation with Sam Bettis that concerns me. We talked about senior management reorganization. Sam asked if I thought you had enough support to get another job in the community. He said he and Jim had been discussing this and wanted my opinion. It's bothered me ever since. Tomorrow I'm going to call Sam and tell him I can't support what he's suggesting."

Lou asked that I call Gary Davis to see if he would back me. I agreed to call. I assured him I did not believe Gary would support my layoff, as Jim had previously promised I would have a job regardless of what was to come.

When I called Gary, he was concerned; he would do what he could. I also contacted Bill Ledford. I was upset with both of them. Neither had fully endorsed me previously; neither had forcefully spoken against my potential demotion. I believed that, had I had Gary's and Bill's leverage and strong backing then, I would not be facing a layoff now. I blamed them for this predicament. They alone could have stopped it.

Bill was genuinely angry about Jim's plan, and he did call. Even though he stepped up, my knowledge that Bill was less than fully supportive had a lingering effect on our relationship. Going forward, I was distrustful of Bill. I was suspicious of Gary too, but I needed whatever support he would give. I had learned Gary tended to play an issue both ways.

The next day, Lou talked to Sam Bettis and then reported back to me.

"I told Sam I couldn't support your layoff, that you were the only one at the hospital who was not a 'yes man' to Jim Whitlock. Keeping you on would not be an issue with Sam, but he said as the administrator, it's Jim's decision."

"That's technically true," I conceded. "However, when it concerns the administration, the Board of Trustees has always been involved in personnel decisions. No administrator has ever gone against the board's wishes."

In a few days, Lou called me again.

"I've circulated my plan to ask for Jim's resignation among most of the board members. Unfortunately, there is no sentiment with any of them to even discuss the issue now. They want to see how the layoff goes first and then assess where we go from there. Good luck and watch your back."

On June 29, the layoffs became public. Fifteen employees out of a total of twenty-seven came from my departments. I met with each of the fifteen, a process that took all day. It was one of the most challenging days of work I had ever experienced.

Back in my office, I got a call from a reporter. He had heard "through the grapevine" that I'd been laid off. I surmised one of the plotters had tipped him off before finding out it wouldn't happen. I had the satisfaction to say that it was not so; it was just a rumor. He thanked me and hung up. I thought, *Maybe I should have said, 'No, they didn't lay me off, but it wasn't for lack of trying.'*

That day, after all the layoffs happened, one of my peers made this statement. "Until right before the layoff, I thought it would affect the whole hospital from the top down, but later I learned it wouldn't."

Another said, "Some of the things did not happen that we planned."

I had stymied the conspirators, at least temporarily.

❖ ❖ ❖

On July 6, I got my new assignment from Jim. After a thirty-day transition, my only responsibilities would be compliance, risk management, and hospital accreditation. These were staff functions for which I was already responsible. My other responsibilities, line management duties, went to the five senior managers in the reengineered administration. I would report to Ken Jackson, the chief financial officer, but keep my assistant administrator title, at least for the next six months. I took the news very calmly and asked very few questions. It was what I had expected.

I expressed no disappointment about my change of duties, but others did about theirs. Doug Renz, the former senior manager who had cursed me and who had heaped the most flattery and fawning on Jim, felt betrayed. He could not understand why the CIO would not be a part of senior management. He believed Jim had deceived him. Doug thought Jim had assured him he would remain in the top tier. He left the hospital in disgust shortly afterward. Others left too.

As for me, I was in jeopardy now more than ever. I felt targeted. Jim would blame me for all the hospital's legal woes that would soon become public. I had to decide what to do next, and quickly.

❖ ❖ ❖

After the layoffs, rumors ramped up about investigations of the hospital. I asked Mike Callaway what he knew.

"Something is up with the district attorney's office regarding HealthWorks and Jim," he said.

Mike Callaway's disclosure led me to entertain the idea of going to the district attorney's office to offer my cooperation. I thought, *What do I have to lose? I certainly have firsthand knowledge they could use.*

The rumors continued. Some board members began circulating news that an investigation of the hospital had begun. Some of the laid-off employees reported local investigators had interviewed them. New county commission chairman, Mike Smith, said he was aware the hospital was under investigation. Mike had succeeded Bill Ledford after the 1998 election. Bill remained on the commission. The new hospital pathologist said he knew a hospital investigation had started that could result in one or more individuals' indictment on federal charges.

Bob Sain acknowledged to other members of the Board of Trustees the FBI had interviewed him. One board member told me he was aware of a "friend" the FBI had interviewed, which I felt had to be himself. The director of the Ocoee Health Alliance said she had supplied information to local authorities.

Gary Davis began calling me and requesting documents. He asked for a copy of the Ramsey Group's contract and the declaration of intent between the hospital and HealthWorks. From these requests, I suspected Gary was directly cooperating with investigators.

He soon confirmed that the local district attorney general's office had interviewed him, and Jim Whitlock and several physicians were under suspicion. He was also cooperating on other matters under investigation, things he did not tell me.

What Gary did not say, which I found out later, was that he had been the subject of one of district attorney's probes. It had to do with a mailing he had sent out during his campaign. Donna Hubbard gave evidence the hospital had used its bulk mailing permit to mail out the letter on his behalf. If this were true, it would be a violation of the law for both Gary and Bradley Memorial. As it turned out, the permit did not belong to the hospital but to the company that did the hospital's mass mailings. Gary had used the same company. Thus, the bulk mailing permit had appeared on both his and the hospital's postings that Donna Hubbard had given as evidence. Investigators completely exonerated Gary and the hospital. Since I had worked at the hospital and for Gary's campaign, I assumed I had been under suspicion too.

By July 14, Jim Whitlock believed I was cooperating in the ongoing investigation. Once this became evident to me, I decided to meet with investigators.

❖ ❖ ❖

In my new role in the hospital, I worked exclusively on compliance efforts. Much of the job was computer-based, putting elements of a plan together using a compliance plan template from Compliance Concepts, Inc. Jim and his new senior management team were suspicious of my work. They feared I was developing a plan that could expose them and the hospital to financial and legal trouble. They plotted how to stop me.

I attended relevant committee meetings, those dealing with specific elements of compliance. Not having to worry about managing departments gave me all the freedom I needed to tailor a plan detailed to Bradley Memorial. I moved ahead as quickly as possible. The timeline set earlier in the year by Jim for board approval was September. I intended to make the deadline.

I discovered that Jim planned to slow me down. Jim and his team would not meet with me. They ignored my email messages and memorandums. Jim would not answer the questions I sent through Ken Jackson. The entire group shut me out. I heard not a word.

One of the few times I saw Jim, we did not want to talk about compliance. He wanted to talk about my mood.

"Michael, you haven't been your old chipper self lately. What's wrong?"

I just stared at him.

❖ ❖ ❖

While I did not answer as to my state of mind, I knew Jim's. By mid-August, the investigation was growing, and he was nervous. He asked Gary Davis to come to the hospital to meet with him privately. At the meeting, Jim asked what Gary knew about the probe. Gary asked Jim how he learned of his involvement, and it turned out that Sam Bettis had told him.

"Michael, I called Sam to let him know, as a courtesy to the board chairman, that this investigation was real, and it was deeper than anyone had imagined. Sam called Jim at once. That's not something you'd expect the chairman to do if the administrator is under investigation."

Gary declined to speak about the subject matter investigators had discussed with him. He did tell Jim that the inquiry was comprehensive. After saying he would not share specifics, Gary told Jim one thing they had asked him. It was about the Ramsey Group contract with the hospital.

Jim also talked about my performance. He expressed his profound disappointment in my work and said I showed a lack of enthusiasm for my new responsibilities. Jim said I had not been very cooperative.

Gary and I agreed Jim was setting me up.

I did not tell Gary I was meeting with investigators. I thought the best way to keep it secret was not to tell anyone, not even my closest allies.

"Jim believes I'm cooperating with investigators. He wants me gone."

Gary agreed.

It was Gary's encounter with Jim that ignited the sequence of events that began in September. On September 27, Jim offered me six month's severance pay if I would leave the hospital quietly. That offer came two days before the meeting of September 29, when Jim placed me on paid administrative leave. After that, the Board of Trustees' executive committee met on October 6, 1999, to decide my fate.

CHAPTER
10

My first meeting with investigators was on July 21. I met with Detective Brian Smith and Assistant District Attorney General Steve Crump. Brian was the lead investigator on the case and brother of the county commission chairman, Mike Smith. He worked for the Cleveland Police Department. Steve Crump worked for District Attorney General Jerry Estes, an elected officeholder. The tenth district, which Jerry represented, was a multicounty region. Steve worked in the Bradley County office. Due to my former position as Chairman of the Bradley County Republican Party, I had known Jerry for many years and worked for his reelection.

Steve Crump said the case against Jim was strong. Since I was a hospital insider, he was eager to get my cooperation.

The investigation was vast, and by the time I became involved, it had been underway for quite some time. Investigators did not tell me, but from what State Senator Jeff Miller had told me during his campaign, I knew the local probe had started in 1998. It had begun with Donna Hubbard's complaint regarding HealthWorks, and it had expanded from there. Investigators asked me to cooperate in a search warrant raid of the hospital for documents. The operation would occur soon. I agreed to help. Over the next several months, I met many times with Brian Smith, Steve Crump, other members of the Cleveland Police Department, the FBI, and the Tennessee Bureau of Investigation (TBI).

The federal investigation originally began with reviewing the hospital's pneumonia upcoding issue, which was a civil matter. From there, it had grown into a criminal inquiry and expanded to include a broader review of Bradley Memorial's Medicare and TennCare policies.

The Ramsey Group contract was also part of the probe. Further, the investigation was looking into issues about the new medical office building. They were also looking at specific insurance arrangements involving the Ocoee Health Alliance. I told the investigators all I knew about each of these issues. After my interview with the TBI, they issued subpoenas for the Compliance Concepts, Inc. risk assessment document that detailed many billing issues. They also issued warrants for home health records.

The local investigation centered on the hospital's status as a public hospital and violations of the law that applied to it the same way they did to all governmental entities.

Leading the list was HealthWorks. I thoroughly briefed them on everything I knew, which was a considerable amount, including the declaration of intent Jim signed with that company. Steve Crump asked me to get investigators a copy of Bradley Memorial's expenditure policy and a second policy that limited what the administrator could purchase without board approval. I gave them these documents. I also answered questions about the hospital's agreements with the Ramey Group and Compliance Concepts, Inc.

There were many other areas of inquiry, and at the heart of them were graft (i.e. the use of a public employee's authority for personal gain) and kickbacks. I had answers for some inquiries but knew nothing of some others.

I was asked: *Did a certain Chattanooga-based construction company* (they named the company) *perform work on Jim Whitlock's, Sam Bettis's, Craig Taylor's, the nursing director's, or Bill Ledford's homes?* I did not know the answer to this question, but I thought: *So, that is why Sam is so desperately supporting Jim. He fears indictment too.*

Did a certain local contractor (they named the contractor) *perform work for hospital employees? Did the hospital give free home health services to Bill Ledford? Did the previously named Chattanooga-based construction company overbill the hospital for construction materials? Did a certain local landscape company* (again they named the company), *contract to do work at the hospital and perform services at Jim Whitlock's house?*

Did hospital maintenance workers do work at the homes of Jim Whitlock, Bill Ledford, Craig Taylor, other hospital employees, or former employees? Did they build a handicap ramp for Bill Ledford? Did Dan Cooper order any of this work?

Dan was director of engineering and was on the hospital's senior management team. Although he was from East Tennessee, he had worked in South Carolina before applying for the job at Bradley Memorial. Since both were mechanical engineers, Sam Bettis and Dan Cooper quickly became friends and allies. Their relationship enabled Dan to join senior management. Sam had always protected Dan and enthusiastically supported his initiatives. I had always been suspicious of Dan. Shortly after arriving, he had set out to take my job. After the effort failed, he apologized, but I never trusted him after that incident. Because of his relationship with Sam Bettis, it was not surprising that prosecutors were asking questions about Dan Cooper.

"Bill Ledford told me hospital maintenance had come to his house to fix his hospital bed," I revealed.

Did information systems employees perform work on computers at Jim Whitlock's home?

"One person told me he did such work." I named the individual.

Did Jim Whitlock's secretary, Juanita Burris, perform work for Bradley

Florist, a small business owned by Jim, while on duty at the hospital?

"Juanita complained to me about having to do their bookkeeping."

Do you know how the same type of slate flooring used in the hospital's medical mall ended up on the floors at Bradley Florist?

"I don't know."

Were Bradley Florist records removed once Jim suspected the investigation included Juanita for bookkeeping work for his floral business?

"Yes. Someone told me records began disappearing from the hospital once the scheme surfaced." I named the individual.

Do you know any hospital employees doing course work for Jim Whitlock in connection with his dissertation?

"Yes. Three different managers told me they had completed papers or other course work for Jim. Another person told me they typed his dissertation." I named those individuals.

Investigators asked me about the Bradley Healthcare Foundation. *Do you know of any misappropriation of funds? Does Jim Whitlock have an ownership interest in the Ocoee Health Alliance? Did Jim Whitlock accept a Florida vacation from David Zimmerman?*

Did Jim's wife wreck a hospital car that insurance refused to repair? Was it later fixed with hospital funds? Did the hospital's home health agency provide services for Whitlock's wife without billing for them?

What role would Larry Ingram and the Home Health Director have in writing off home health bills? Larry was the senior manager responsible for the hospital's home health department.

"Each would have the authority."

Other questions centered around Zimmerman & Associates, the Dave Gordon engagements, and the hospital's office supply contract. I told them as much as I could.

The probe was looking at all hospital senior managers. Investigators specifically focused on Larry Ingram. They believed he was going out of his way to help Jim and hinder their work. Because of his actions, Larry could face a charge of accessory after the fact.

Over the next several months, hospital management and board members accused me of having started the entire investigation. They were unaware the probe had begun long before my cooperation.

CHAPTER
11

There was a lot of activity in the days and weeks that followed my suspension. The story eventually emerged for the public through Gary Davis's and others' political maneuverings. As the investigation intensified, Gary began his political attack, and Jim Whitlock and his supporters counteracted with a massive disinformation campaign. The legal probe and the politics surrounding the issues ran along separate but parallel lines that sometimes seemed to intersect.

Jerry Estes, usually content to let his prosecutors manage cases, took on this one personally. I never directly discussed the investigation with him. I knew it was inappropriate. However, Jerry had to instruct Mike Callaway that no one associated with the hospital, including board members, should call him about the case. Several of them had already tried. No one would pressure Jerry.

Records began disappearing from the hospital. Larry Ingram entered my office, even after a warning by investigators not to, and removed boxes of my personal papers. Still on paid administrative leave, I had no way to prevent it. Employees reported that another senior manager left the hospital with two large briefcases. It was alarming, but the long-anticipated raid never came.

Talk of an imminent indictment was all over the hospital. In response, Jim set out on a "walk around campaign." Suddenly, he was all over the hospital, more visible than ever talking to employees and reassuring them. Jim said that everything was fine and any rumors they were hearing were unfounded.

The senior managers began spinning the investigation as nothing more than political. They enlisted some of their supporters in the community to reiterate the same sentiment.

When necessary, Jim tamped down opposition within the hospital through intimidation. Jim called Dan Cooper to his office, where he met Jim, Dewayne Belew, and the human resources director. Dan told me about the conversation. Jim asked if Dan had talked to me, to which he answered yes. He told Jim he had called from home and the conversation was personal. Jim next asked if Dan knew of any information being spread around about a certain Chattanooga-based construction company (he named the business). Dan said he did not have any knowledge of it, and he was not involved with any kind of investigation.

Regarding the incident, Dan told me Jim was on a "fishing expedition." He was incensed by Jim's questions and for being "hauled" in for questioning.

Because the investigation had become widely known, federal and state agents showed up at the hospital with a subpoena for records instead of executing a raid. Their arrival rattled Larry Ingram. Larry told investigators he had only been a "go-between." He believed Jim would sacrifice anyone to protect himself. Larry's concerns, however, did not keep him from asking a pointed question to the TBI agent: "Who is responsible for this probe?" The agent just stared at Larry without answering.

As it became known that the authorities were interviewing maintenance employees, a further sense of panic set in at Bradley Memorial. The news spread throughout the hospital, further complicating efforts to tamp down the rumors.

Gary's political assault was a crucial step, as the news media and the public were unaware of what was going on. Gary, through his actions, set out to alter that.

Gary formulated a plan whereby I would issue a sworn statement to the press, setting out all I knew about Jim's indiscretions. I met with Mike Smith to give him a rundown of all the issues. He, too, advocated I publish a statement. I agreed to do it but told both that I preferred another approach, if possible. I had not yet given up hope of returning to the hospital. Gary also enlisted the help of Dan Cooper to write a similar letter and suggested I might obtain the support of Bill Ledford in this strategy. I declined the suggestion. I had no confidence that Bill would support me. I drafted a statement and gave it to Gary for his review. I did not know if Dan Cooper supplied one, but I believed he backed out. Gary told me he was going to hold my statement for a few days.

Jim began meeting with community leaders to gauge their support. Rumors were spreading that he had locked me out of my office and fired me. It was certainly true that I had been locked out of my office, and while I had not been fired but rather placed on paid leave, Jim was having an awkward time explaining each incident.

Jim also suspected the Bradley County Commission would soon take up the hospital issues. He wanted to get opinions and reactions from those he considered close friends and allies.

He met with former administrators Howard Kuhns and Bill Torrence. He strategized extensively with Sam Bettis, Mike Callaway, Larry Ingram, and Dewayne Belew. Bill Torrence told me about his meeting with Jim.

"You need to know what Jim told me. He intends to let you go eventually."

I was not surprised, but it saddened me to know that my career there was probably ending. Still, I was determined to continue fighting.

Larry Ingram continued assailing my and Craig Taylor's performances about compliance issues by saying in meetings that neither of us had "done much with compliance." Compliance Concepts Consultant Steve Spargo went with Larry to these meetings to legitimize Larry's accusations. They handed out the risk assessment document to managers at the center of the controversy and asked them to begin addressing the issues in it. Blame for the hospital's compliance issues had started shifting to me.

Gary chose not to use my sworn statement but to issue a letter, in which he used some of the wording from my original statement. He addressed his letter to the Board of Trustees but did not make it public. Anxiety soon skyrocketed within the hospital administration and board regarding how to address the letter.

Gary received feedback from two board members. Bobbie Atchley said that Jim Whitlock should resign. Sam Bettis told Gary the board agreed not to take any action against Jim until or unless the grand jury issued an indictment.

"The district attorney advised us to do nothing for now, but if the grand jury indicts Jim, we'll ask him to resign."

From conversations with investigators, Gary and I knew Sam's statement was false. It was another outrageous lie.

The letter made its way to the news media by an anonymous source. Neither Gary nor I had sent it. It was fortuitous that the circumstance played perfectly into Gary's strategy. The letter urged the trustees "for a vote of confidence or the resignation of Jim Whitlock."

Gary commented when the *Cleveland Daily Banner* asked him for a response. "As county executive, I have a big responsibility to assure that all of Bradley County's interests operate for the good of the people. Bradley Memorial Hospital is one of our greatest assets. I continue to support this great institution to the best of my ability. I recently encouraged the Board of Trustees to safeguard Bradley Memorial Hospital as a public asset in private correspondence. I asked that during these challenging times, they assure themselves and the public, of strong and effective leadership."

The newspaper asked for Sam Bettis's response. He said the board would not ask for Jim's resignation without first receiving legal counsel.

The *Cleveland Daily Banner* article went on to state that "one of the issues is the supposed suspension of Michael Willis, former assistant administrator and risk management employee." Dewayne Belew affirmed I was on paid administrative leave. Because it was a personnel issue, he could not comment on the reason. It was the first time my status in relation to the legal issues surrounding Bradley Memorial Hospital had been the topic of public discussion.

The article supplied the public spotlight needed for the politics of the matter to move forward.

The day the news article appeared, I got a call from the publisher of the *Cleveland Daily Banner* to come in for an interview. I agreed to an off-the-record meeting. I spoke with the publisher and editor. After telling them why I was on administrative leave, I informed them of everything I knew about the criminal investigation. I felt confident in this, as Steve Crump had told me I could talk about anything of which I had firsthand knowledge.

❖ ❖ ❖

I also explained Gary's strategy. He raised the leadership issue as a proxy to reveal the criminal probe, which the district attorney general's office had not yet acknowledged. His way of placing pressure on the hospital and the local investigation was to get it into the public arena. The publisher and editor expressed their compliments of Gary's strategy and promised vigorous coverage going forward. The editor said he would contact Jerry Estes for comments.

A few days later, Mike Smith called to ask me to give him the sworn statement I had written for Gary; it was now time to move with it. I was hesitant, just as I had been with Gary. I suggested an alternate strategy that used Gary's current public letter to the Board of Trustees. Why not announce that the Bradley County Commission was considering a resolution of no confidence in Jim Whitlock's leadership of Bradley Memorial Hospital?

Mike liked my idea but went with a different strategy. Instead of a resolution addressing Jim Whitlock's status, Mike invited both Jim and Sam to come before the county commission to discuss all the rumors and uncertainty swirling about the hospital. It was an opportunity to get the investigation acknowledged in a public setting, something the district attorney general's office had not done.

As the next county commission meeting approached, the investigation intensified. It was a deliberate strategy. Brian Smith notified many individuals of their impending sworn interviews, including the board members. Brian also made plans to interview Juanita Burris and Larry Ingram. Many of these meetings occurred over the next several days. Brian intended the interviews to show the investigation's visibility and seriousness, pressure potential witnesses, and force Jim Whitlock's resignation.

The senior managers defended Jim at a department head meeting. They asked if anyone had any questions about the article in the newspaper.

Furthermore, they went on to attack Gary Davis. Senior managers were disappointed in Gary. After supporting his bid to become the county executive, he had now turned against the hospital.

In response, a department head observed how curious it was that Jim couldn't get along with the county executive—first Donna Hubbard, and then Gary Davis. The senior managers did not appreciate the comment.

I became a topic of discussion. A senior manager disparagingly cut the topic short by saying my case was a disciplinary issue, and it was inappropriate to discuss it.

Many reported that Jim Whitlock "looked dreadful."

A few days before Jim and Sam appeared before the county commission, two articles appeared in the *Cleveland Daily Banner* on the same day about Bradley Memorial Hospital. One reported the county commission's request for Jim's and Sam's appearances and the ominous implications. Juxtaposed against the first article, the second one reported THA's official announcement that Jim Whitlock had received the Meritorious Service Award for CEO, an award he had won earlier that June. The difference between the two pieces could not have been starker. Later, this award discredited Gary Davis's motivations because the nominating application included his letter of support.

The night of the county commission meeting, Jim was a no-show. Conrad Finnell, a well-respected local criminal defense attorney, attended in his place. Conrad announced that his client, Jim Whitlock, had been advised not to answer any questions at that time due to an investigation by the police department. He went on to say, "We understand that the Cleveland Police Department has interviewed at least two employees and three board members, and at this point, we don't know what the investigation involves."

Dewayne Belew followed up to say, "The hospital wants to remove any questions or rumors that may be circulating and address them *factually.*"

Neither the Cleveland Police Department nor the district attorney general's office would confirm or deny the reports, which was standard procedure. But with Conrad Finnell's revelation, there was finally no plausible deniability. The issue was now public.

After Conrad's disclosure, the news media overlooked much of the rest of the county commission meeting, but not the investigators in attendance. In answer to a question, Sam Bettis admitted that Jim had violated a hospital policy when arranging a loan to HealthWorks. The loan did not have board approval. Hospital board guidelines dictated that they had to approve any expenditure over ten thousand dollars.

After the meeting, the news coverage exploded. The *Chattanooga Times-Free Press* picked up the story, as did the *Associated Press* and all four Chattanooga television stations' newsrooms. The information made its way across Tennessee, and I helped fuel it.

A FOX 61 news reporter came to my house to see if I would do an interview. Still on paid leave, I was outside in my flower beds when he arrived. I was hot and sweaty from planting winter pansies. I declined the interview, but the reporter agreed to an off-the-record conversation. I deliberately used it to stoke the news. I told him about the possible misappropriation of funds involving HealthWorks and Jim's secretary performing work for Bradley Florist while she was on duty at the hospital. I also told him I addressed questions centered on misdirection of public funds and kickbacks, such as hospital work at Jim Whitlock's, Sam Bettis's, and Bill Ledford's homes. I gave the reporter a picture of Jim from the *Bradley Post*, an employee newsletter. It produced a grainy image on television. From my perspective, it was perfect.

The reporter was excited. I would be an "unnamed source." He ran the scoop—the first to penetrate the untold tale. He asked for directions to Bill Ledford's and Bradley Florist, and off he went. The story broke that night. It was huge. All the other Chattanooga stations then clamored to get their news.

My decision to include Bill Ledford was not a mistake. I knew including him in the report would create a media sensation, and I thought, *There's not a chance Bill will get indicted, but it will cause him embarrassment—a small price to pay.* It may also have been a tiny bit of payback for not supporting me as vigorously as I thought he should have.

The next day, Gary and I discussed the previous night's meeting. He said, "Conrad Finnell's statement left no doubt that Jim is under criminal investigation. I believe the county commission and I can now stay out of the matter and let the investigation go ahead. I am pleased with the outcome. Things will settle down now." They didn't.

The senior management of the hospital was in a panic. At the department head meeting, Jim told the group he could not make any comments due to his attorney's advice, but he was doing fine. He said he had experienced some sleepless nights, but he was hanging in there. He told the group he would not resign.

One senior manager asked how one disgruntled employee could cause all the trouble.

Another said someone went outside the hospital's grievance process to address problems.

Yet another indicated that the issue was purely political. They noted the irony of Gary Davis attacking Jim when just a few months back, he had nominated him for an award.

In the days after the county commission meeting, Brian Smith continued taking sworn statements from hospital employees and board members. Now was not the time to ease the pressure. I wrote a series of questions for Brian to ask in his interview with Dan Cooper.

During this time, Bradley Memorial Hospital also held an event to celebrate the previous ten years of accomplishments. This celebration coincided with Jim Whitlock's ten-year anniversary as the administrator. Everyone in attendance noticed my photographs were conspicuously absent in the timeline of achievements.

"It's as if you'd never existed," a department head told me. "How can they rewrite history?"

When an attorney representing Conrad Finnell approached Brian

Smith, I got my first sign that Jim was finally breaking. He asked if Jerry Estes would be willing to drop all charges in exchange for Jim Whitlock's resignation. Brian said he did not think so but would inquire to the district attorney general's office. Over the next few days, others contacted the office as well. Jerry was angry. His response was, "Absolutely not."

Jim Whitlock resigned at the Board of Trustees meeting on November 22. It came less than two weeks after Conrad Finnell's disclosure of the investigation to the county commission. Less than two months had passed from the time Jim had challenged me to pull off his ouster if I could.

Gary gave me advance notice about Jim's decision, which he had heard from Lou Patten. Gary said he planned to attend the meeting. Jim Whitlock's resignation would not be immediate, staying on until his tenth anniversary as the administrator, December 31. Also, before Jim's departure, the board would appoint an interim administrator.

Lou asked Gary if he would support Don Lorton for the job. Gary categorically said no. Lou argued over the issue, but Gary said it was inappropriate for any board member to be considered for the job.

Lou went on to inform Gary I could not return to the hospital because of all the strained relationships. Gary disagreed with his assessment, saying that everyone who worked in the administration should have a chance to prove themselves, including me.

In his resignation to the board, Jim said the Cleveland Police Department's recent inquiries about himself or the hospital had no bearing on his decision to resign.

"The Cleveland Police Department has been conducting an inquiry for more than six months. There is no sign when they will conclude their investigation. Consequently, my decision to change positions should not interfere or affect this ongoing process. I will be happy to cooperate to whatever extent requested, regardless of the state of my employment."

Jim announced his intention to teach at Brenau University in

Gainesville, Georgia, as the head of the Health Care Management Program in the Department of Business Management and Mass Communication. He had completed his postgraduate degree in healthcare administration at the Medical University of South Carolina in Charleston during the summer of 1999, so this career change was possible. He also planned to consult in the healthcare field with Zimmerman & Associates.

Despite Jim's measured, prepared statement, Bob Sain conveyed an exact sentiment of the board. He said publicly, "Some say what comes around goes around. I hope that for these people who have given us problems, their time will come."

Bob was talking about Gary, the investigators, and me. It was a sinister statement, one that did not bode well for my return to Bradley Memorial. His comment, along with Lou's to Gary, were consistent with what other board members said and what I had heard from Bill Torrence.

Gary's comments were surprisingly complimentary of Jim that evening despite his letter that had pushed Jim to this moment.

"I would like to say I think Jim has done an excellent job. He had a vision when he started, and he's worked toward that vision and accomplished a lot."

Gary's comments came despite the hospital's loss of $6.4 million in the previous fiscal year and an expected loss of $5.8 million in that current fiscal year. He was trying to have it both ways.

The next day, Jim Whitlock addressed a somber department head meeting. It was short. Jim said he had planned to teach eventually. Only the timetable had changed.

❖ ❖ ❖

Jim's resignation set off a scramble within the hospital to replace him. Sam Bettis had intended to name Larry Ingram as the interim administrator at the board meeting. Lou Patten, Don Lorton, and Bobbie Atchley opposed the plan. That opposition left the situation in limbo. Instead, Sam announced they would decide on an interim administrator later.

Over the coming days, the board continued to square off into two competing camps. Sam and his group stood by Larry Ingram, while Lou and his group offered two alternatives—Don Lorton or Don Lorton overseeing the senior managers who would serve collectively as the interim administrator.

When these alternatives failed, other names were offered but none were acceptable.

Dan Cooper, seeing all the chaos around the selection, postured to become the interim administrator. After his bid was also rejected, Dan concluded he had no future at Bradley Memorial Hospital.

Finally, as a compromise, board members agreed to hire an interim administrator from outside the hospital. An active search began. My outcome, whichever way the board elected to go, was final. In a call to Gary, Don Lorton said I would be unable to return to Bradley Memorial. Relationships were too strained. To make the point clear, Bob Sain followed up his public comment with a private conversation. He told Bill Torrence he would not support my return either.

❖ ❖ ❖

In the days following Jim's resignation, Bradley Memorial's public image continued to erode as another controversy erupted over a rumor that the hospital board was considering a severance package for Jim. The community inundated county commission members with questions.

County commissioners asked Gary if the hospital board had settled.

"There is a lot of talk on the street," Gary responded, "but I know no more than what they discussed at the November 22 hospital board meeting."

One county commissioner asked if Jim Whitlock could legally get a severance package since he'd resigned. Another said his constituents were asking questions, and he could not give them any answers.

County Commission Chairman Mike Smith stated, "All I'm hearing are rumors, but I'll ask Sam Bettis and report back to the commission. I know there is no mention of any discussion of a severance plan in the hospital's minutes. If they have already approved a plan, it violates the state's open meetings law."

Another county commissioner suggested the possibility of dissolving the hospital board altogether if its members were not any more responsive to the public than they appeared to be.

Gary later discussed the matter with Sam Bettis, who said the board had authorized him to work out a severance deal with Jim. It would pay the difference between Jim's new job pay and his current hospital salary for two years. Sam said he planned to present it to the Board of Trustees at their next meeting on December 27.

The final approved package consisted of a maximum of $130,000 per year for two years, plus health insurance. The announcement incensed the county commission.

"He doesn't deserve it," one said. "He resigned. When you leave from any position, you are not supposed to have severance pay."

"I want to check on it and see if it's legal or not," said another. "That's my concern. I don't think it's legal."

"That's county money, and I don't care what kind of deal they made with him."

For the second time, county commissioners discussed the possibility of passing a resolution to dissolve the hospital Board of Trustees.

❖ ❖ ❖

The next day, December 28, 1999, Larry Ingram announced during an afternoon department head meeting that the hospital had abolished my position. My employment with the hospital had ended. My last day of service would be December 31. The hospital would require me to answer questions about my activities in an exit interview with Mike Callaway. I was at home, still on paid leave, when I learned about this announcement from an informant before I got an official notification. It came later by certified mail.

The elimination of my job was a last resort effort by the hospital to keep me from filing a lawsuit. When Jim had placed me on administrative leave, he employed attorneys to find a way to fire me for-cause. They looked to see if anything I had done violated any rule or regulation. The activity reviewed included my disclosures to board members, Gary Davis, county commissioners, and law enforcement. The lawyers scoured the employee handbook and the state and federals laws seeking at least one violation. Their review found nothing. A for-cause termination could have potentially forestalled a whistleblower lawsuit. They now hoped eliminating my job would serve the same purpose.

Gary talked to Lou Patten about my termination. Lou said I would get one month's severance pay and attend an exit interview with Mike Callaway. The board had asked Jim Whitlock to deal with my situation before leaving, something he was glad to do. Lou said he supported the action.

"Michael, it's time for you to contact an attorney," Gary said.

Jim Whitlock had fired me on his last day of employment at Bradley Memorial Hospital.

CHAPTER
12

In January 2000, Gary gave me the personal telephone number of Jimmy Logan Jr., a prominent criminal defense attorney in Cleveland, Tennessee, and a behind-the-scenes political operative. He was a Democrat, but most attorneys in the community were then. I knew Jimmy a little but knew *about* him a lot. Jimmy Logan was considered the best lawyer a defendant could get.

Jimmy was the son of Jimmy Logan Sr., who had served as the county's Register of Deeds as a Democrat during the era before Bradley County's transformation into a Republican stronghold. To Republicans, Jimmy was a Yellow Dog Democrat. It's a term from the nineteenth century that applied to voters in the South who voted solely for Democrats. Allegedly, these voters would vote for a yellow dog before they would vote for a Republican. The term has largely faded from use today, with Jimmy Logan being an exception.

Fortunately, I had never needed Jimmy Logan for any criminal matters. Gary suggested, however, that I could use his political expertise as I navigated what had become a political and legal minefield.

Even though Jimmy was a Democrat, he cultivated relationships with all politicians, elected and otherwise, Democrat or Republican. Most of his connections were with Republican officeholders, as very few Democrats held office in Bradley County. While I'd been Chairman of the Bradley County Republican Party, I had kept Jimmy at arm's length. That was about to change.

I took my letter of termination to Jimmy. He was already aware of the situation, and he agreed to help. Jimmy felt the legal route would be challenging, and my best chance hung on a political solution. The key to reinstatement was Mike Callaway and whatever recommendation he made to the board. We agreed that taking the issue public should be part of the strategy. Jimmy drafted a letter to Mike Callaway.

As the next county commission meeting approached, it was clear the public debate over the hospital would continue. After Jim Whitlock's resignation, two Chattanooga hospitals, Memorial and Erlanger, gave county commissioners proposals, offering to manage Bradley Memorial. Community Health Systems had also proposed a fifty-million-dollar, twenty-five-year lease. Infuriated by Jim Whitlock's severance package, members of the county commission also planned to introduce a resolution calling for all the hospital trustees' resignations. The hospital remained at the center of a growing political firestorm.

Sam Bettis reviewed the management and lease proposals. He said, "The board has said for a long time that they are not interested in leasing or selling the hospital."

His comment angered the two county commissioners most interested in pursuing the propositions.

The county commission introduced a resolution calling for the resignation of the Board of Trustees. The vote failed on a seven-to-seven tie. Bill Ledford led the opposition, which was another sign I could no longer count on him. The closeness of the vote highlighted how divisive the issue had become.

Mike Smith publicly invited Sam Bettis to appear at the next meeting. He wanted a public discussion of the proposed hospital management and lease bids. Mike also wanted Sam to answer why the county commission should not again take up the board's resignation.

At its next meeting, the county commission voted to hand off to a committee composed of both county commissioners and trustees the proposals on the hospital's management or lease. By that time, the Board of Trustees had selected John Barnes, a former Erlanger executive, as its interim administrator. Sam Bettis and the entire Board of Trustees attended the meeting.

At the session, the discussion continued about Jim Whitlock's severance package. Sam Bettis added a new wrinkle to the debate by claiming Jim had not resigned voluntarily, triggering the payout requirement as prescribed in his contract. This admission outraged county commissioners. They accused Sam of deception. Sam said it was just a misunderstanding. County commissioners introduced a second resolution calling for the resignation of the Board of Trustees. It again failed on a tie vote.

Sam Bettis addressed other issues that night. He answered questions about HealthWorks. County commissioners asked Sam about the medical office building lease, employees doing work on homes of individuals associated with the hospital (including county commissioners), pneumonia billing, and hospital losses. Investigators had intensified their probe after Jim's announced resignation, so they were in the room listening.

One commissioner reportedly asked, "Was Mike Willis fired for telling the truth?"

Sam Bettis's reply was both disparaging and defamatory. Sam sarcastically asked the commissioner who he was talking about, as though Sam didn't know me. He then mockingly remembered that there had indeed been someone at the hospital by my name who had done extremely poor, part-time work. Investigators attending the meeting were shocked. They told me I probably could sue for slander.

The next day, in retaliation for the county commission introducing a resolution twice calling for the board member's resignations, Larry Ingram and Dewayne Belew tried to organize a petition to remove the members of the Bradley County Commission. They started it despite the fact there was no provision in the Tennessee Constitution for a recall election. It garnered little support and only served to heighten the animosity. Their political strategy miserably collapsed.

County commissioners did not give up after their second failed vote that called for the hospital board members' resignations. Motivated by the recall petition, over the next few years, as their terms came up for renewal, three of the four appointees from the county lost their jobs. Bobbie Atchley was the only one reappointed. The medical staff also replaced their representative on the board.

The Cleveland City Council helped too. When Don Lorton's and Lou Patten's terms came before them on the same day for renewal, the council replaced them. Don Lorton, who by then was chairman of the Board of Trustees, was shocked and bewildered as to how it could have happened. Lou was serving as the vice-chairman. The hospital board scrambled to name new leadership.

Herbert Lackey was one of the new county appointees to the hospital board. An old foe from the past had reappeared. It was the same Herbert Lackey I had competed with to become the assistant administrator back in 1984. He would soon be giving me trouble again.

❖ ❖ ❖

After the county commission meeting, I got a call from the *Cleveland Daily Banner*, then met with the publisher and editor again. While they had not printed Sam's remarks about me, they offered to let me supply answers to the questions surrounding my termination at Bradley Memorial Hospital. If I wrote a letter to the editor, they would print it on the front page, an extraordinary placement. I agreed, and the article appeared in the newspaper on January 14, 2000.

The letter was lengthy, but one paragraph served as the heart of what I wanted to convey to the public.

In July 1999, I was requested to and began cooperating with legal authorities regarding certain matters under investigation at the hospital. I discussed this investigation's nature with the hospital's legal counsel and the Board of Trustees through the hospital's legal counsel on Oct. 8, 1999. Jim Whitlock insisted on placing me on paid administrative leave until the Board of Trustees completed a review. The hospital's legal counsel assured me I would be returning to work once authorities settled these matters. However, instead of getting my job back, I received a notice of termination by a letter signed by Jim Whitlock during his last week at the hospital. The letter advised me that Jim Whitlock had ended my position at the hospital, effective December 31, 1999.

After the newspaper published my letter, Jimmy Logan completed a letter to Mike Callaway. He copied and sent it to each hospital board member seeking a settlement for "wrongful discharge." I hand-delivered them to Mike Callaway's office and hospital administration.

While Jimmy prepared his letter, I worked on a disclosure naming every legal issue I was aware of at Bradley Memorial Hospital. This document served as my exit interview. I cited forty-six problems, which Jimmy cut to thirty-seven. He believed I should not tip off the hospital about nine of them. I hand-delivered the letter to Mike Callaway.

When I presented the disclosures, Mike Callaway asked me to meet later with an attorney with Compliance Concepts, Inc., to go over the document. I declined, saying, "This meeting constitutes the exit interview. I won't be meeting with anyone else."

It did not take long to hear back from the hospital on the requested settlement. Interim Administrator John Barnes quickly denied my appeal. He asked me to return my name tag and any hospital property I had in my possession and retrieve my personal belongings. I complied. The human resources director aided me—or more accurately, watched over me carefully—as I did.

When I later talked to Brian Smith, he told me he had two hospital employees' sworn statements that completely contradicted the public statements made by Sam Bettis at the county commission meeting. Regarding HealthWorks, Brian said Sam's statements could prove he engaged in "official misconduct."

❖ ❖ ❖

The investigation of Jim Whitlock and the hospital intensified. Interviews of employees continued. After Sam Bettis's county commission remarks, Brian issued eight more subpoenas for hospital employees' sworn statements. Later, he issued five more. The Bradley County Grand Jury also issued warrants for home health records.

As I had done for other meetings, I prepared a series of questions for Brian Smith and a TBI agent to ask Larry Ingram during his sworn interview, which John Barnes and Mike Callaway attended. Regarding pneumonia upcoding, Larry said the only person who could have authorized any changes to codes was the medical records director. Brian was concerned because Craig Taylor had told him the same thing at his interview. I assured Brian that the director could not have done it; she did not have the authority.

Brian asked me if I knew someone who could get a message to the director to tell her about Larry's statement. His purpose was to get her cooperation; otherwise, she might not be a willing interviewee. I told him I knew someone who would do it and could not be associated with me.

I prepared a script and gave the friend the medical records director's home telephone number. When he made the call, her husband answered instead. The director was not home, so my contact left a message. When asked, he gave his name as Jim.

The director of medical records was outraged. She went to John Barnes at once, who then called Larry into the meeting. Of course, Larry could not deny what he had said. John had been sitting at the conference.

The director believed Jim Whitlock had been the one to warn her. The truth of the matter, though, was that my colleague, rattled when asked for a name, randomly picked the name Jim. He had not expected the question, and it was a poor choice. He had not made a conscious attempt to associate the call with Jim Whitlock.

I called Brian to say that the director was now probably eager to cooperate, which she did. He was happy.

❖ ❖ ❖

After my termination, I started the challenging task of looking for work. I applied to various hospitals and other healthcare providers both locally and regionally. As rejections began to pile up, it became clear that I was being blackballed. I expanded my search to the national level, and a few interview requests came in. I was not eager to move.

The CEO of Cleveland Community Hospital called me. He was one individual to whom I had not sent a resume. He asked me to see him; he wanted to interview me. I agreed but was suspicious. I thought it probable the CEO was only trying to pry information from me, which was correct. My interview was more like an inquiry. I left disgusted.

❖ ❖ ❖

On March 20, Carl Shrewsbury, the man Gary Davis had beaten in the primary election, resigned as Gary's executive assistant. Gary asked if I would be interested in the job. I told him I would consider it. I was hesitant to leave the field of healthcare, believing I still may have a future there. Going into government would probably make such a future choice unlikely. Still, over the next few weeks, we discussed and negotiated the terms. Since the job paid only about half of what I'd made at the hospital, I would also have to get support from my wife. She was reluctant at first but finally decided she did not like the idea of moving either.

The job description encompassed several duties. My job title was Executive Assistant to the County Mayor. In this role, I would work with Gary on issues to go before the county commission. I would also write his letters and speeches, stand for him on various boards and committees, and stand in for him at community functions that he could not attend.

Other duties included serving as the county's risk manager. It was a similar role I had played at Bradley Memorial. Responsibilities also included developing the county's personnel budget, organizing a human resources department, and rewriting the employee personnel handbook. These, too, were duties I had performed at the hospital.

Because of the adverse public spotlight at Bradley Memorial, I did not look forward to the prospect of attending ribbon cuttings and community functions. I wanted to keep my head down. Such events would make me feel awkward, conspicuous, and ill at ease. But these duties were part of the job, and I would have to adapt.

An unwritten duty in my work for Gary was to help him get reelected. It was the most important task, from his standpoint. He wanted me to immerse myself in the politics of Bradley County, to keep my eyes and ears on what was happening, to stand for his interests. Gary asked me for a two-and-a-half-year commitment if I came to work for him, which would see him through the 2002 election.

I agreed to the terms with one warning. "At this point, I don't know if it will happen, but I reserve the right to sue Bradley Memorial Hospital."

Gary expressed his concern about my stipulation but agreed to the possibility. He knew if I filed a lawsuit, it would become very public, a prospect Gary did not like. As one who always played both sides of an issue, it would cast him clearly on my side.

Hospital officials greeted my hiring with nervousness but soon devised a plan to deal with it. Within a few days, Larry Ingram and Dewayne Belew expressed lovely comments about me and my new role in the hospital meetings.

Later, Dewayne sought me out at a county commission meeting he attended.

"I hope you don't think I had anything to do with your leaving the hospital. It was an issue just between you and Jim."

"Dewayne, I know the story of how things happened."

He replied in a sharp tone, "Are you implying that *I* had something to do with it?"

"Again, I know the *whole* story, the *complete* story. I know every person who was involved." I referred to the secret meeting held by some of the senior managers to discuss my potential lay-off.

"I had nothing to do with it," he reiterated.

"Then you don't have anything to worry about, do you?" I replied.

Dewayne puffed up, shook his head, and walked off.

CHAPTER
13

My first day of work as Gary Davis's executive assistant was April 17, 2000. The county commission met. They greeted me warmly. It was an emotional day, as I had not expected to be there. My focus had been on returning to Bradley Memorial, not to Bradley County. My head was in a whirl as I tried to absorb the new reality. It seemed like an out-of-body experience. Even though I felt these emotions, I was thankful to be working again. After what I had been through, I had been unsure I would ever find other work, especially in Cleveland, Tennessee. I was grateful for Gary's confidence in me.

The press approached me curiously, got the information they needed, and ran newspaper articles on Gary Davis's new executive assistant. They highlighted my experience at Bradley Memorial Hospital but did not reference the controversy there. I was appreciative.

I returned to a county government hugely different from the one I had left two decades before. Of course, all the officeholders were new, but there seemed to be a different atmosphere about the place. There were not as many shady people hanging around. Elected officials were much more involved in running their offices instead of leaving them to subordinates.

That did not mean there was not some wastefulness, just not as much as I had seen in my earlier years.

Gary Davis's county executive office was dysfunctional from a staffing perspective. After his election, Gary had kept all of Donna Hubbard's office staff, including Carl Shrewsbury. Gary had taken a cautious approach upon assuming office, believing that firing the existing staff would have been very detrimental to him and his new administration. He needed their skills. Gary decided to let each prove themselves. If they caused political trouble, he would deal with them after he had found his footing. He soon learned that the staff was in fact going to be trouble for him.

I was surprised when, after his election, Gary told me he would keep Carl Shrewsbury. They had run bitter campaigns against each other. Gary had beaten him by only fifty-three votes. How could they get along? Even though there was tension between them, somehow, Carl stayed for a time. Now he was leaving. Rumors circulated that Carl planned to mount another campaign against Gary. No one knew for sure. It was clear, however, that he was going to work as the sheriff's budget director. Gary was glad to see him go. He believed Carl was leaking sensitive information from the office.

Although Gary had not pressured Carl to leave, he saw it as the first of three needed changes. The other staff left within a year after my arrival.

A few days after I had started my new job, I got a call from Lou Patten to congratulate me. I was cordial. I suspected he was trying to make amends because his company wrote insurance for Bradley County. I was now in charge of it.

Dan Cooper came by to congratulate me. We made small talk. He asked questions about my role in the ongoing investigations of the hospital and Jim Whitlock. I evaded answering. I was confused about his motives, but the questioning led me to believe that Dan was recording our conversation. If he was, he got nothing.

I visited with Bill Ledford, a long-delayed meeting. Bill was a key ally of Gary's on the county commission, and it was essential for us to reconcile. He told me I should have come to see him sooner. I replied that I had been too upset with him, and it would not have mattered anyway. Jim had his ear. We settled our differences and moved on. It was best for both of us.

Gary Davis was a fiscal conservative. He believed in balancing the budget every year without a tax increase. Gary's approach appealed to the public. In her last year in office, Donna Hubbard had presided over the most significant property tax increase ever. Gary pledged not to let it happen again. The tax increase was one reason Donna had chosen not to run for reelection. During the seven years I worked for Gary, he never proposed a property tax increase and always presented balanced budgets to the county commission for approval.

To be fair to Donna Hubbard, the Tennessee General Assembly had virtually mandated the property tax increase to equalize education spending across the state. Some counties, like Bradley County, were getting a disproportionate share of state dollars. The state government took the excesses from larger counties and gave them to the smaller ones. The funding shift left a big hole in Bradley County's education budget. The county had to decide to either increase local funding or cut education spending. Bradley County chose to fill the funding gap with a property tax increase. Donna, of course, had proposed the sale of Bradley Memorial Hospital to use the proceeds to fund capital school projects, which would have reduced the size of that tax boost.

Through the years, Gary's no-tax-expansion philosophy worked only because of the tremendous growth rate in the county's property and sales taxes. As the county's population increased, so did home, business, and industrial construction. Adding these new parcels to the tax rolls generated new revenue. Added people also meant more spending on goods and services, which increased sales tax revenue. The growth in the number of people moving to Bradley County more than offset its budget increases. Gary's proposals always had sizeable reserves.

Gary Davis was one of the luckiest politicians ever. His good fortune allowed him to concentrate exclusively on getting reelected. In the years I worked for him, Gary easily won reelection in 2002 and 2006.

Whatever decisions Gary made in his role as the county executive always related to winning the next term of office. The day after his victory in 2006, Gary said, "I know it's a terrible thing to say, but I'm already thinking about reelection in 2010."

Gary's conservative philosophy also extended to other areas besides budgeting. His leadership style was one of leading from behind. Whether it was industrial parks, new schools, or new roads, Gary always stayed in the shadow of the issue until he saw how the public reacted. He stayed away from controversial matters while embracing popular ones, even taking credit for the successful ones he had not originally championed. It was Gary's goal to never get on the wrong side of an issue.

Some unpopular issues he opposed publicly but supported privately. The development of the new Cleveland Regional Jetport is a case in point. Bradley County had needed a new airport for more than twenty years. The city's municipal airport was small and outdated. The city invited the county to join them in building a modern facility. It was a highly unpopular proposal in rural Bradley County. These residents saw it as nothing more than a place for millionaires to park their toys. Gary knew something his rural base did not. The area boasted the fifth-biggest industrial base in Tennessee, and many Fortune 500 companies had industrial plants in the county.

Bradley County was beginning to lose new industrial recruits because of its outdated airport. Gary opposed joint funding. His fiscal conservatism made him reluctant, given that the city was likely to build it anyway without the county's help. He also knew rural voters opposed the airport, and that these voters favored him disproportionately. They were Gary's base. His opposition was popular with them.

The City of Cleveland moved ahead but bought land outside the city limits. It would take county approval to adopt the zoning changes and approve an infrastructure plan. Behind the scenes, Gary helped city leaders navigate the politics of the county commission and win approval. Gary Davis's name will never be on a building at the new airport, but his quiet support helped make it a reality.

My philosophy of government was a little different from Gary's. While I shared his fiscal conservatism, I believed the county executive should lead the county forward. Some issues were worth advocating regardless of their popularity. It was up to the county executive to persuade and spearhead improvements for the county.

Sometimes our differences of philosophy clashed. Those times were frustrating. Even though Gary was fiscally conservative, there were a few county departments that enjoyed excess funding. I encouraged Gary to look at them, but he would not. There was political risk involved.

The Cleveland/Bradley County Emergency Management Agency (EMA) was one of these. I reviewed their budget and looked at their operation and found them overstaffed. There were four staff positions, including the director.

The EMA Director served as a coordinator of government agencies, public safety officials, nonprofit organizations, and city and county officials during emergencies or natural disasters. This coordinator wrote all emergency response plans and procedures for this purpose.

For the size of Bradley County, I recommended only one and a half EMA positions: the director and a part-time secretary. The preferred structure was to share a secretary with another department. There was not enough work for four people. Gary opposed the change, as it would put him at odds with the emergency responder community.

They could pose a threat to his reelection.

The EMA was also an overfunded agency. In addition to local funds, it got federal grants. They also got money from the Tennessee Valley Authority (TVA) to prepare for potential disasters at the nearby Sequoyah Nuclear Plant. Bradley County sat within a thirty-mile radius of the TVA facility, which mandated specific planning and drills. The EMA was awash in cash, which meant they had the best and newest equipment, vehicles, and technology. Some of the buying was necessary, while other things, such as mounted television sets in each office, were excessive. Since they had a lot of free time on their hands, the staff watched television a lot.

Shortly after coming to work for Gary, I began work on his reelection campaign. Planning began more than a year and a half in advance. I organized a biennial County Executive's Dinner and made calls for donations. Gary's opponents soon began complaining.

"How can you work on Gary's campaign from your county office? It's illegal, Michael Willis."

It was not. Tennessee has a unique law that applies only to local elected officials. There is no legal prohibition to them using their offices and staff for campaign purposes. If they want, an officeholder can set up a campaign headquarters in the courthouse. There are strict rules on the state level prohibiting such conduct. Gary and I knew the law, but I began making the calls from home to stem the criticism.

At times I intimidated Gary's potential challengers, but in a legitimate way. One rival had been attending county commission meetings for months to gather information in anticipation of challenging Gary in the Republican primary.

Meanwhile, I attended a back-tax committee meeting. I discovered the man's name listed among those owing the county back taxes on their property in the discussion. It was an accidental finding, but I used it.

I commented on the problem the next time I saw him. "Do you think it's a legitimate public concern if certain candidates for county executive haven't paid their taxes?"

"Ah, ah. I've always paid my taxes."

"You better check with Chancery Court to be sure."

I never saw the man at another county commission meeting, and he did not run for county executive.

CHAPTER
14

As the months of 2000 passed, the investigation at Bradley Memorial Hospital began to feel distant. I got updates from Brian Smith and, when asked, continued to work with him on various aspects of the probe. But after Jim Whitlock's departure, the investigation seemed less intense and slowed to a crawl. It was like emptying molasses from a mason jar. Watching the thick syrup pour out was exasperating.

Brian asked me to write up questions to ask Jim Whitlock for his sworn interview. I completed a lengthy list.

Brian called Conrad Finnell to set up the meeting. Conrad refused a face-to-face interview but said his client might be willing to give written answers to questions. Brian mailed them. Conrad wrote back saying the entire investigation was political, and his client would not be taking part.

By November, when it seemed the case would go before the Bradley County Grand Jury, Brian had me help prepare a synopsis of the investigation for him to present. Still, the case did not go.

I never imagined such a long delay. Several months in a row, investigators said charges were going to the grand jury *next month*. But when the next month came, there still were no charges. It was frustrating.

Assistant District Attorney Steve Crump attributed some of the delays to the federal investigation.

By August 2000, after repeated attempts to reach a settlement on my behalf with Bradley Memorial, Jimmy Logan said it was time to file a civil action. There were no options left. The strategy was to wait until the last minute to allow the grand jury to hear Jim Whitlock's case. An indictment would bolster my case.

Earlier, Jimmy had been optimistic he could negotiate a settlement in the fifty-thousand-dollar range. It would include an apology from the Board of Trustees. The amount was lower than I had expected, but it was a settlement offer instead of a lawsuit. John Barnes had agreed to thirty thousand dollars, but the board rejected it and authorized him to counter with only a "pittance," as Jimmy described it.

Partly to blame for this failure were the ongoing negotiations surrounding HealthWorks. Jimmy represented one of the physicians involved in the joint venture with the hospital. HealthWorks attorneys had discovered what they believed was a flaw in the declaration of intent Jim Whitlock had signed. If disputed, Bradley Memorial stood to get nothing. They offered $394,000 to settle. It was the amount the physicians had received from the sale of the business to Columbia/HCA. The completion of the deal would come at the end of August 2000.

John Barnes rejected the offer on the grounds that it paid only seventy cents on the dollar. He could not take such a settlement to the Board of Trustees. They would accept nothing less than full payment. He believed the press and the public would crucify the hospital. John Barnes and the board thought the same thing about settling with me. (As it turned out, in 2004, the hospital finally resolved the HealthWorks litigation for $300,000, which was $94,000 less than the original offer.)

We waited on the grand jury to act, but by the end of the year and approaching the one-year filing deadline, my civil case had to move forward. On December 8, 2000, Jimmy introduced me to Harry Burnett, a Chattanooga workplace employment attorney. I agreed to let Harry handle the lawsuit. He was the best attorney to handle this kind of litigation. I filed a civil action for wrongful discharge in the Chancery Court of Bradley County on December 27, 2000.

The Chancellor recused herself from the case, as did every judge in Bradley County due to personal conflicts of interest. I knew all of them and had helped them in their campaigns for office. The case assignment went to a judge from Chattanooga.

I filed the lawsuit under the Tennessee Whistleblower Act, a law that gives employee protections on the state level in a way that is comparable to how federal law governs federal workers. Under the statute's general provision, an employee may not lose their job for refusing to participate in illegal activities or revealing unlawful activities. The law protected every activity I had undertaken at the hospital. It was a mystery how the entire board and management of Bradley Memorial Hospital could dismiss it.

My case filing finally revealed details never known to the public. The Chattanooga and Cleveland press extensively covered the lawsuit. Disclosures included the claim that I, the plaintiff, lost my job "solely because [I] refused to remain silent about illegal activities." The filing followed up with details and sought "unspecified damages for lost wages and the value of Willis's employment benefits from the date of his termination, as well as additional compensatory and liquidated damages, including damages for humiliation and embarrassment, pain and suffering, and emotional distress." I also sought damages for deprivation of my civil rights and attorney fees.

My attorney prepared a carefully worded statement for me to make to the media. "The majority of my adulthood has been dedicated to the enrichment of the quality of life in Bradley County. More specifically, this has been through my employment with Bradley Memorial Hospital. The hospital terminated me because I cooperated with the investigation into matters which are critical to the lawful, orderly discharge of the responsibilities of Bradley Memorial Hospital to its patients and the community. I have attempted to deal with this professionally and will continue to do so. Because this matter is pending in our state courts, I will be unable to comment in greater detail at this time. It is time that the facts incident to my termination be open to public scrutiny in a forum where the truth is determined. It is the only way for justice to prevail."

Gary got nervous once the lawsuit became public. He did not like the newspapers referencing the fact I was now working as his executive assistant. Gary wanted me to issue another statement saying that the lawsuit had nothing to do with my current employment. Later he changed his mind after receiving mostly favorable feedback from the public.

CHAPTER
15

As 2001 arrived, Jim Whitlock's formal charges might have followed just after I filed my lawsuit but for two issues.

The first involved my civil action. The district attorney general's office did not want to issue the indictment in the same month I filed my civil case. It would look like we had coordinated the two actions. Also, I had named Steve Crump as one of the potential witnesses. He knew the facts and circumstances surrounding my litigation subject matter. Steve was not pleased with me for having listed him and said the grand jury's presentation needed to wait until he had time to review my lawsuit. I told Steve that Harry Burnett, my attorney, had wanted him on the list. It would be an incentive for the hospital to settle. Steve was willing to testify, but only after Jim Whitlock's criminal case. The long-term effect of naming Steve Crump as a witness was to place my civil litigation behind the criminal one.

The other problem involved politics. Vetting had begun for two individuals, including District Attorney General Jerry Estes, under consideration for United States Attorney for the Eastern District of Tennessee by the then-new George W. Bush administration. Federal background checks and political considerations stretched out the review process. As jockeying between the contestants for the Bush appointment was underway, members of Jerry's staff also maneuvered to be his successor. The two main rivals were Steve Crump and another assistant district attorney, both from the Bradley County office. I agreed to help Steve secure the appointment if it came. As a result of the political posturing, neither Steve nor the other assistant district attorney was anxious to pursue the highly controversial Jim Whitlock case until the Bush administration decided on Jerry Estes' appointment. In the end, the President did not nominate Jerry. Still, the internal political maneuvering delayed the grand jury presentation for months.

Brian Smith continued to update me. In June 2001, he told me the grand jury would soon hear a presentation, but then corrected himself and said it would go in July. He later changed it to August because Jerry Estes wanted more records from the hospital. They would use the July grand jury to issue subpoenas for them.

These subpoenas again shook Bradley Memorial's senior management. Their feelings were raw.

A confidant told me that in a hospital department head meeting, senior managers discussed these latest subpoenas. One senior manager reportedly said, "I hate Michael Willis."

To which another apparently replied, "Amen."

Another senior manager showed interest in obtaining a copy of the case file from investigators once the investigation concluded. He said ominously, "I want to know what was said by *every employee* interviewed."

On August 2, I met with Steve Crump and Brian Smith to discuss the grand jury presentation. On August 7, I met with Brian to review the final six-count indictment. I was surprised but did not say anything. From my knowledge, I knew there had been many more areas of investigation. What had become of those?

The Bradley County Grand Jury met in session on August 8, where

Brian presented the Jim Whitlock case. The grand jury published the true bills on August 13. They returned a six-count indictment, the same ones we had discussed. The news media was ready. Jim's case quickly made headlines both locally and throughout the state.

I helped make sure. On August 8, I prepared media packets with all the relevant background information, alerting the local press outlets about the true bills, which the grand jury would hand down on August 13, 2001. I mailed them anonymously. Within a few days, I was getting requests for interviews. I declined and cited my civil case as the reason. I did, however, offer to speak off the record to any reporter who requested an interview.

The grand jury summoned Jim Whitlock to criminal court on August 13 for the reading of the indictments. Only Conrad Finnell, who had required an upfront payment of one hundred thousand dollars from Jim to take the case, showed up for court. Conrad waived Jim's right to an arraignment. Sheriff's deputies booked Jim at the Bradley County Justice Center later that morning. They took Jim's mug shot and fingerprints. Media outlets used this picture in their coverage. I took no comfort in seeing these events unfold even though I realized there was a measure of vindication in them. It was sad to know that if Jim had simply acted ethically, he could have avoided all the trouble he'd brought on himself and the hospital.

"Even though we didn't request a specific monetary amount in your case, the value just went up," said Harry Burnett when he heard the news.

The six felony charges included one count of theft over sixty thousand dollars from Bradley Memorial, one count of theft of services over one thousand dollars from the hospital, and three counts of official misconduct. There was also one count of coercion of a witness.

The felony charge of theft over sixty thousand dollars violated hospital policy by arranging a $564,000 loan to HealthWorks. The theft of services charge was for Jim diverting services to his benefit—home health care services for his wife.

The first official misconduct charge was for Jim vacationing in a condominium in Naples, Florida, which belonged to David Zimmerman, obtaining a hospital consultant's benefit. The second charge was for Jim having his hospital secretary do bookkeeping work for his private floral business, Bradley Florist. She did this accounting during her hospital work hours while receiving pay from Bradley Memorial. The third charge was for Jim's unauthorized exercise of official power by terminating the employment of me, one Michael Willis.

The final charge was unlawfully and intentionally, by coercion, influencing or trying to pressure me, a witness in an official proceeding.

While deputies at the justice center booked Jim, Conrad Finnell was talking to the press. He put the best spin he could on the situation. "Jim is not guilty, and he's maintained his innocence from the very beginning. We all know this investigation has been going on for a long time. We all know that grand jury proceedings are ex parte. The defendant does not appear and has no representation by counsel at this point. There is only one witness on the face of the indictment, and that was the investigating officer. These are serious allegations, and we will handle them as such."

Steve Crump also addressed the same assemblage of reporters. "This has been a long-running investigation. The grand jury wants us to review some specific things, but the investigation is complete."

Steve's statement referenced a hidden grand jury request. After hearing Jim Whitlock's case, angry grand jurors ordered a follow-up investigation of the hospital. They wanted to know if it was possible to indict others. The grand jury requested the district attorney general's office come back at a future session with more information. They wanted to know who else was involved.

Not the Bradley County Grand Jury foreman nor any other grand jury member could reveal any information from their proceedings under penalty of law. The foreman, however, told me about the grand jury's request. "If you tell who tipped you off, I'll deny it."

There had been a total of fifteen counts that the district attorney general's office had allowed the statute of limitations to run out. This revelation had troubled the grand jurors, prompting their request.

While local authorities were announcing Jim Whitlock's criminal case, the United States Attorney for the Eastern District of Tennessee announced a civil settlement. It was obvious by the timing that the federal and state announcements had been coordinated.

The federal civil settlement pertained to the long-running Bradley Memorial Hospital pneumonia probe. They did not report any federal criminal charges. In addition to the United States Attorney's Office, the federal departments involved in the investigation included the Inspector General's Office, the Federal Bureau of Investigation, and the Department of Health and Human Services.

In the settlement, the hospital agreed to pay $1,792,033 back to the federal government for over-reimbursement for treated cases of pneumonia. They also signed a corporate integrity agreement that included a code of ethics, self-auditing on coding issues, and a two-person team to assign codes. It required regular reports to the federal government and compelled the hospital to allow future audits. In exchange, the federal government did not assess fines, fees, or damages, which could have increased the hospital's payback tenfold.

In one whirlwind week, all the issues I had dealt with for the previous two years were finally out in public. I had mixed emotions. Even though the pneumonia upcoding case outcome had been predictable, I was aware of many more billing issues from my review of the compliance documents. The federal government did not address any of these. I also wondered what had happened to the criminal part of the federal grand jury case in Chattanooga.

As for the local allegations against Jim Whitlock, I was glad investigators had finally brought charges, but I was disappointed too. There should have been others. Why had the district attorney general's office not acted earlier to include more indictments? They were aware of the statute of limitations. I was annoyed but dared not express it. The district attorney general and I would need each other to prosecute Jim Whitlock successfully.

❖ ❖ ❖

During the months following Jim's indictment, Conrad Finnell introduced various motions that stretched out the legal proceedings and delayed the trial.

In September 2001, Conrad approached Steve Crump about allowing Jim to plea to a misdemeanor. Through Brian, he floated the idea to me to get my reaction.

"If Steve asks me directly, I'll react negatively," I said. "I'd be happy with a felony plea, though."

"This offer of a plea deal puts Steve in a tricky situation," Brian replied. "He wants to run for public office, and he wants to handle things right."

"I want Steve to run for office too, and I want to help him, but he also needs to help me. If he helps me, I'll help him."

It was the most hardened stance I had taken since the beginning of the whole affair. Steve did not strike a deal.

In October 2001, Steve met with officials of Bradley Memorial Hospital. Mike Callaway asked him to attend a meeting that also included Don Lorton and Administrator John Barnes. By then the Board of Trustees had removed "Interim" from his title. The discussion lasted about five minutes once Steve discovered the reason for the conference. Don demanded to know if the prosecution was politically motivated, which offended Steve. Steve explicitly said there was no political motivation. The decision to present the evidence to the grand jury was his and his alone. Steve said he intended to prosecute Jim Whitlock fully.

Later in October, Conrad Finnell filed a motion in the Criminal Court of Bradley County to dismiss the first count of the six-count indictment.

In the motion, Conrad included a memorandum. "The grand jury returned an indictment on the sole testimony of Cleveland Police Department Detective Brian Smith. He is the brother of the county commissioner, Mike Smith, who publicly expressed dissatisfaction with Jim Whitlock and the administration at Bradley Memorial Hospital. We believe this relationship to be inconsistent with an unbiased investigation of the facts and representative of a significant conflict of interest in the testimony to the grand jury. We believe this testimony happened because of political hostility. It resulted from the defendant's successful blocking of the county executive's attempt to sell Bradley Memorial Hospital to outside interests and the continuing public attacks on the hospital between September 1996 and November 1999."

The county executive reference was to both Donna Hubbard and Gary Davis, referencing Donna's attempt to sell the hospital when she was in office and Gary's letter asking for a vote of confidence or the resignation of Jim Whitlock.

Conrad Finnell did not want to file this motion; he did not want to argue a political motivation. He did so only at the insistence of Jim Whitlock.

In November 2001, the criminal court judge declined to dismiss the charge. He set a tentative trial date of May 22, 2002, which was later rescheduled to August 1, 2002. He ruled in favor of a separate trial for HealthWorks, which would happen first. Also, the judge granted Conrad Finnell's motion for three separate trials. They would follow afterward.

The second trial grouped charges involving the personal enrichment of the defendant. It included the Zimmerman vacation in Florida, book-keeping services performed for Bradley Florist by a hospital employee, and the diversion of home health services to Whitlock's wife. The third trial included the charges involving me, the official misconduct charge for ending my employment, and the allegation of a witness's coercion.

It was clear from Conrad's memorandum that Jim blamed the HealthWorks financial transactions on Craig Taylor and the deal itself on Mike Callaway. In it, Jim blamed Craig, saying, even though he was the administrator, he was unaware of the wire transactions. Jim blamed Mike because he prepared the contract that authorized the payments as the hospital's attorney.

❖ ❖ ❖

While these matters were playing out in criminal court, the fore-man of the Bradley County Grand Jury, one of Gary Davis's most prom-inent supporters, met with Gary. He told Gary of a deal he had struck with Lou Patten. Rumors had circulated for months that Lou was going to challenge Gary in the Republican primary in 2002. Talk accelerated after Lou sold his interest in his insurance company to free himself for the race.

The foreman's deal with Lou was to drop any further grand jury investigation into Bradley Memorial Hospital in exchange for an an-nouncement that he was not running for county executive. It was an at-tractive offer for Lou, who most likely feared the exposure of his having sold insurance to the hospital while serving on its board. As the Grand Jury Foreman, this man had the power to make it happen. Lou accepted the offer, and the grand jury took no further action.

Gary Davis's fear that Carl Shrewsbury would oppose him in 2002 did not come to fruition either. Gary easily won the May 7 Republican primary and the August 1 general election. He faced only token opposition in each race.

As I'd promised, I helped Gary get reelected. It was my primary duty for much of 2002. I served as his campaign coordinator and treasurer, organizing groups and committees, and conducted fundraising.

CHAPTER
16

There was no significant movement in my case until 2002, a year after I'd filed the whistleblower lawsuit. In March, Harry Burnett filed fifty pages of answers to interrogatories, the most extended responses he had ever presented. The answers were long because I had to answer many complex questions about my role as the hospital's compliance officer. I also had to detail my efforts to implement a plan, what I had found in my compliance reviews, and to whom I had reported them. It took fifty pages to supply complete answers and a long time for me to construct them.

My deposition occurred in May 2002. It lasted five hours, including a short break for lunch. The hospital's insurance carrier, the same company I had worked with for many years as the hospital risk manager, had appointed the hospital's attorneys to question me. I had also worked with other lawyers at their law firm. Even though I was not an attorney, they knew I was knowledgeable, especially in legal proceedings. They would handle my deposition carefully. The defendant attorney's goal is to trip up the plaintiff, to get them to say something to get the case thrown out on summary judgment. They failed in their efforts to trick me into making contradictory statements or admit opposite facts.

The agreement between Harry Burnett and the hospital attorneys was to have Jim Whitlock's deposition follow mine. It did not happen. Conrad Finnell resisted because August 1, 2002, was his client's trial date. Harry's strategy was to schedule the deposition before Jim's trial. It would put pressure on the hospital to settle. Harry tried to serve a subpoena, but Jim's new address could not be found to serve it.

In late July, I received a subpoena to appear in Jim Whitlock's first trial. At the time, the district attorney general's office intended to try all three cases regardless of each outcome. Jim was not eligible for pretrial or judicial diversion. Gary Davis got a subpoena too.

Regardless of what I'd previously believed, Steve Crump did offer a plea bargain before the trial. Perhaps it was the felony plea deal I'd suggested, but I don't know since I was never consulted. Apparently, though, it was not acceptable to Jim because the parties did not announce an agreement.

For political reasons, at the last minute, Steve continued the case to October 17, 2002. The August 1 general local election and state primary prompted the delay. First, the trial would be uncomfortable for Gary at a time he was on the ballot. Second, it would impede Steve's campaign to help a candidate win the Republican primary for the United States Senate. He was the candidate's Bradley County chairman. If Steve helped this person win, it would boost his political standing. Steve wanted to use the time to concentrate on the race. In the end, Steve's candidate ended up losing the primary.

❖ ❖ ❖

After I filed my case in Bradley County Chancery Court, hospital attorneys filed a motion to move the case to federal court in Chattanooga. They believed they could get a more favorable ruling there. The Chattanooga state judge overseeing the case approved the request.

Hospital attorneys were able to secure this change because the lawsuit raised a constitutional issue of free speech. They argued the federal courts should decide the matter. The First Amendment claim was a long-shot move on Harry's part, but he believed it was still significant. He said it was almost impossible to get a favorable ruling in federal court on free speech rights. A United States district judge dismissed on summary judgment the First Amendment issue and sent the rest of the lawsuit back to Chancery Court for trial on the whistleblower questions.

"We consider this a victory," Harry Burnett said in a statement to the press. "It was Bradley Memorial Hospital that wanted this in federal court in the first place."

As to the dismissal of the First Amendment claim, Harry said, "It was not at all a loss because ninety-eight percent of the lawsuit is still intact."

Dewayne Belew, now working for John Barnes, issued a written statement characterizing the judge's ruling as "an endorsement of what we were saying all along that these charges have no merit. Our goal from day one has been to have all the questions answered and to let justice prevail."

Dewayne spun the decision as a win for the hospital, even though the judge denied summary judgment on the whistleblower charges.

Chancery Court set my trial for September 30, 2002. Steve Crump filed a motion to suppress his testimony and that of Brian Smith, which delayed the matter indefinitely. This motion didn't surprise me since Jim Whitlock's trial was set to begin about the same time.

❖ ❖ ❖

On October 16, I met with Steve Crump to go over my testimony. He told me I would be the first witness. Steve would give me a two-hour advance notice to appear.

I was uneasy with the trial from the start; uncomfortable with the charge—theft over sixty thousand dollars. There had been a total of 564 thousand dollars *misappropriated*, but stolen? A better allegation was official misconduct. That claim was something the public and jurors could understand. Many public officials had gone to jail for misappropriating less.

Once prosecutors realized they let slip the one-year statute of limitations on official misconduct for HealthWorks, they went with the theft claim. A theft charge was their only choice to keep the count alive. If prosecutors had charged misappropriation of hospital funds instead of theft, along with the five other counts, it would have provided a more durable corruption case. Furthermore, if they had sought an indictment earlier, adding the other fifteen expired counts would have created overwhelming evidence of public fraud. But the district attorney general's office had set the charges. I would answer the prosecutor's questions and do all I could to help.

At the beginning of the trial on October 17, Harry Burnett sent his paralegal to watch the court case from start to finish. He was interested in gathering useful information for my lawsuit. We were not disappointed.

On the first day, it took only two hours to complete jury selection. There were eight men, four women, and four alternates. Following this process, Assistant District Attorney Steve Crump read the charges. Jim Whitlock pleaded not guilty. Next, opening statements were to begin for the prosecution and defense. However, the criminal court judge announced an unusual delay in the proceedings. He would hear from attorneys in his private chambers. It meant I would not be testifying that day.

On October 18, the next day, the judge revealed he had granted Conrad Finnell's motions heard the previous day in his chambers. Conrad did not want jurors to know Jim Whitlock had gotten a severance package. Also, he did not want jurors to know which witnesses for the prosecution were testifying under immunity. The second request was highly unusual. Most defense attorneys want jurors to know of immunity agreements.

There were two practical motives for Conrad's request about immunity witnesses. He did not want it revealed that I had no immunity. I had never believed it necessary, so I had never asked for it, and investigators had never offered it. Some of the hospital senior managers had tried to implicate me and gave what proved to be false information to investigators in their quest. If prosecutors had revealed I had no immunity agreement, it would have bolstered my credibility, something Conrad was sure to attack.

Conrad's second reason was the possibility that Craig Taylor had immunity for his testimony. I did not know for sure, as I had never asked, but it seemed likely. If Craig had immunity from prosecution, the revelation would implicate Jim since the two of them had been a team when it came to the hospital's finances. They were too closely tied together.

Steve Crump presented the state's case. In his opening statement, he said he would prove that Jim Whitlock had approved the expenditure of money without authorization from the Bradley Memorial Hospital Board of Trustees. He told the jury the case was about responsibility and following the rules. In this case, not following the rules broke the law.

In his opening statement, Conrad Finnell countered that he would prove that the hospital trustees had known of the transaction. Jim Whitlock had not intended to deprive Bradley Memorial of the money; instead, he'd intended to make money from the joint venture with HealthWorks. Conrad also said that the board had granted Jim Whitlock approval in other such joint ventures, and Jim did not think it was wrong to go ahead with this agreement. Conrad insisted that Jim was a visionary who was pursuing a plan that could have brought in millions of dollars for the hospital. Conrad Finnell concluded his remarks by telling the jury Jim Whitlock never personally profited from the agreement.

It was this last statement that would prove decisive to the outcome of the case.

In my testimony, I told jurors Jim was aware he could not spend over ten thousand dollars of hospital funds without board approval. I also testified that Jim had not obtained the permission necessary to transfer funds to HealthWorks.

"He asked me to research board minutes to find out what his spending limit was," I stated. "We thought it was twenty-five thousand dollars, but I found that it was only ten thousand dollars. Jim said that he would ignore the board minutes. If he had money in the budget to spend, he would do so."

On cross-examination, Conrad Finnell tried to attack my motives in testifying for the prosecution. He implied my reasons were jealousy and hard feelings. I had wanted the job of hospital administrator when Jim Whitlock had gotten it. Both of us were assistant administrators at the time and vying for the position.

Conrad asked, "Did it not leave you with some bitterness?"

"Mr. Finnell, I never applied for the job."

Conrad was surprised. He had counted on Jim's faulty memory to score a point. The line of questioning ended.

By the end of my testimony, I had been on the witness stand for most of the day. I began at nine thirty in the morning and concluded at two thirty in the afternoon.

Larry Ingram followed me on the witness stand. He testified about the relationship of the hospital's physician recruitment policies and how they pertained to HealthWorks. Larry also testified about his role in setting up physical therapy and lab services for the joint venture. He answered Steve's questions truthfully, but he did all he could to help Jim's defense under cross-examination.

One of the HealthWorks' partners also testified. His line of questioning centered around the declaration of intent his group of physicians signed with Bradley Memorial.

Finally, Gary Davis testified. When he was on the board, Health-Works was a vague memory. He did not recall its approval.

Under cross-examination, Conrad Finnell asked Gary if his letter to the Board of Trustees calling for a vote of approval or the resignation of Jim Whitlock was politically motivated. Gary answered no. The correspondence conveyed to the board that there were severe issues about Jim's hospital leadership that they should address.

"Mr. Davis, why did you send a letter to the Tennessee Hospital Association in support of Jim's nomination for the Meritorious Service Award for CEO? Were you concerned then about Jim's leadership?" Conrad asked.

In an embarrassing moment, Gary had no answer.

❖ ❖ ❖

After the weekend, the trial resumed on Monday, October 21. Several witnesses testified throughout the day.

Craig Taylor testified for the prosecution. He affirmed that funds had been wired to HealthWorks to keep the hospital board in the dark about the transactions, and these transactions had Jim's full knowledge and approval. Craig said Jim wanted to use wire transfers rather than send paper checks. Paper checks required a countersignature from a board member, while wire transfers had no such verification requirement. Craig also testified that the entire senior management team had discussed the transactions many times at their meetings. Earlier, in my testimony, I had affirmed Craig's claim.

Mike Callaway, the final witness for the prosecution, said his only role was to prepare and execute the declaration of intent at Jim's request. It was not his responsibility to get board approval. It was Jim's.

Conrad Finnell called Sam Bettis as the first witness for the defense, followed by Bob Sain. Both testified that while the board took no formal vote, each was aware of and approved the HealthWorks joint venture. In their testimony, Sam and Bob fully supported Jim's defense.

Finally, Jim Whitlock took the stand. In upholding his actions, Jim mirrored much of what Conrad Finnell had already argued in his opening statement. Hospital trustees knew of the transaction, and it was a way for the hospital to make money. The board had also approved other such joint ventures, and he did not think it wrong to go ahead with this one.

Jim Whitlock then made two good statements in my lawsuit against the hospital, though I'm sure they were not intended to be helpful. He said he'd known I was cooperating in the investigation that led to his indictment, and it had made him angry. He also said the board permitted him to fire me.

The second admission contradicted Sam Bettis, who had said earlier the board left the decision to fire me up to Jim.

I was told we wouldn't need Jim Whitlock's deposition anymore, just a copy of his sworn testimony.

The trial went into the evening. Conrad Finnell made a motion for judgment of acquittal based on the Tennessee Rules of Criminal Procedure. Following more than eighteen hours of testimony, the criminal court judge granted an acquittal on the theft charge against Jim Whitlock. The case did not go to the jury.

Rule 29 of the criminal code says a judge can invoke an acquittal based on the defendant's motion or the court's initiative. It declares the court shall order the entry of a judgment of acquittal after either side closes their evidence. It may do so only if the evidence presented is insufficient to sustain a conviction of the offense. It is a rarely used procedure that is seen as a reprimand to the prosecution for presenting a flawed case.

"The state's proof simply cannot support a conviction that the defendant intended to steal money from Bradley Memorial Hospital," said the judge. "The proof cannot support that the defendant intended to deprive them of that money permanently. The crime of theft requires the taking of property without the owner's effective consent. The state's proof was not only that other people knew the transfer of funds occurred but that other people did the actual transfers."

The case ended as I had feared. The evidence was tailor-made for the charge of official misconduct because it was clear to me that misappropriation of funds had occurred. A jury could have understood that claim.

Conrad Finnell had argued, "This was not theft."

The judge agreed.

While I was disappointed with the trial's result, I was more dissatisfied with the case's prosecution. It should not have ended like this. I wanted answers but had to remain silent. There were still five counts to try. However, I feared that prosecutors might be skittish about trying the others after losing the first case.

Following the acquittal, Jim said he held no ill will toward anyone.

I thought, *Surely that's not true. You hold no animosity toward me, Steve Crump, Jerry Estes, Brian Smith, Mike Smith, or Gary Davis?*

In his statement to the press, Steve Crump said he *might* try the other charges later. His choice of words was foretelling.

CHAPTER
17

S everal events occurred in 2003 that slowed down the remaining charges in the Jim Whitlock case and my whistleblower lawsuit. By this time, I had become exhausted by the whole affair. I could see nothing ahead but dark clouds and a miserable future. My life had sunk into the lowest ditch that could ever be dug.

In February, Steve Crump told me to expect another trial to be set sometime between April and June. He said the second Whitlock trial would involve the two charges involving me, official misconduct for ending my employment and coercion of a witness. However, on April 13, 2003, just six months after Jim Whitlock's first trial, Conrad Finnell died of cancer. Jim chose another respected attorney from Cleveland. By necessity, the transfer of the case files resulted in a delay. The new attorney needed time to review the material and prepare for trial.

In April 2003, Bradley Memorial Hospital's insurance carrier also went into receivership, placing an indefinite hold on my civil case. The delay would last until the Tennessee Commissioner of Insurance assigned attorneys to it. He certainly would reassign the earlier attorneys, but first, there would be a series of legal steps. The Chattanooga judge overseeing my case did not remove her order to suspend action on the case until September 2004, a year and a half later. After that, other delays would postpone the outcome until September 2006, six years after I filed my lawsuit.

In July 2003, Steve Crump told me he would soon set Jim's two remaining trials. For the first time, however, I detected Steve was no longer enthusiastic when discussing the case.

When September 2003 came and the Jim Whitlock trials were still not on the docket, I inquired. Steve said Jim's attorney had approached him about settling the remaining charges. Steve was agreeable to reaching a deal. I was disappointed but did not express it. I still needed Steve's testimony in my civil case and did not want to jeopardize that. Also, Gary had never been enthusiastic about the limelight caused by the Whitlock case. I did not wish for a dispute with the district attorney general's office over a settlement to add to Gary's discomfort. I had no choice but to repress my feelings.

In January 2004, Brian Smith told me Steve Crump was working out a settlement to drop the remaining charges in exchange for Jim Whitlock paying restitution. He did not yet know the amount. Steve said such a deal would still make Jim guilty in the eyes of the public, even if he went without punishment legally.

The settlement came on February 18, 2004. Steve talked to me after the fact. He said Jim would have to pay restitution of $324. The payment was to go to Bradley Memorial to reimburse the time spent working on Bradley Florist's books. David Zimmerman would get four hundred dollars for Jim's use of his condominium in Naples, Florida. Steve dropped the offense of theft over one thousand dollars. The charge was for receipt of unreimbursed home health services for Jim Whitlock's wife. The hospital produced what I perceived as a dubious home health policy that allowed for employee write-offs after insurance filing. I told Steve no such rule had existed at the time of the services. These restitution payments were indeed a pittance. How Steve Crump believed such a settlement was fair was beyond my understanding.

Steve said the two charges involving me were "nolled" (*nolle prose-qui*), meaning the allegations could come before a grand jury again. But that would only happen if Jim Whitlock implicated himself through deposition or discovery in my civil case. Steve said the case file would remain open for my attorney to see. He also told me he would help my suit and be available for deposition. He was hoping to appease me. I thanked him for his help.

In his filing, Steve made a statement about the two dropped charges involving me that was upsetting. "The state cannot prove beyond a reasonable doubt that Whitlock knew of the pending investigations or the cooperation by Willis with any authorities."

Steve's assertion contradicted Jim's sworn trial testimony. Jim said he knew I was cooperating, and it made him angry. I was upset and confused by Steve Crump's statement.

❖ ❖ ❖

In 2006, after Steve was announced as a candidate for district attorney general, he contradicted his earlier assessment that the case file would remain open. He told me the Whitlock records were no longer accessible. The court had expunged (or deleted) them. They would not be available for use in my civil case. My interpretation of this revelation was that, as a district attorney general candidate, Steve no longer was interested in cooperating in my civil case. Later, I discovered his statement about these records was wrong. The Whitlock documents' expungement did not occur until 2010, when Jim's attorney petitioned the court to purge them.

Tennessee law allows for the expungement of court records. It enables the destruction, at no cost to the individual, of all public records of a person charged with a misdemeanor or a felony once the court receives their petition. Expungement may happen only under certain circumstances. For Jim, he could have his records purged because the law allowed it if there was a verdict of "not guilty," whether by a jury or by the judge following a bench trial.

❖ ❖ ❖

The reaction of the public to the Jim Whitlock settlement was predictable. Those who supported Jim were happy. Those who thought he was a scoundrel were outraged.

Jim's supporters used the acquittal as proof that the whole affair was politically motivated. They were amazed at the power I wielded. They wondered how one disgruntled individual could have caused all the trouble. Others wanted to know what I had over Jerry Estes. Some referred to me as a purely evil person.

The Jim Whitlock detractors said his status as a wealthy man allowed him to avoid incarceration and other severe punishment. He could afford the high-priced, legendary criminal defense attorney Conrad Finnell, who helped Whitlock get off. Most people could not afford such an attorney; they would just have to go to jail.

Many distrusted and suspected the criminal court judge, confused about how he could acquit a defendant. They asked why the judge would not allow a jury to decide Whitlock's fate. Others speculated about Conrad Finnell and the judge's relationship and wondered if someone had paid off the judge. Another train of thought suspected Finnell's legal arguments were so deceptive that they thoroughly baffled this particular judge, which then led him to acquit Whitlock.

The public was irate about the settlement with Bradley Memorial Hospital. They saw the fine of only $324 for bookkeeping services performed by Jim's secretary as a mockery. They believed it was a rather good deal for Whitlock.

There was a common belief about the Zimmerman settlement that

Jim's acceptance of a vacation in Zimmerman's luxury condominium in Naples, Florida, was a crime. They said that Zimmerman gave Whitlock the gift in exchange for thousands of dollars for work at Bradley Memorial. They saw the repayment of a mere four hundred dollars for a Florida vacation as an insult to Bradley County's taxpayers. Others said Zimmerman probably turned around and gave that money back to Whitlock.

Some speculated about the cases involving me. They wondered why Steve Crump would say he couldn't prove beyond a reasonable doubt that Jim Whitlock knew of the pending investigations or my cooperation with any authorities. Critics asked why Crump had charged Whitlock in the first place if he couldn't prove it. They also said all a person needed to do was hear my testimony to know I was telling the truth.

A general sentiment resulting from the Jim Whitlock case was that another person in a comparable situation needed to get their hands on as much money as they could. It was the only way to get off if they were guilty as sin.

CHAPTER
18

D uring 2004 and 2005, while my whistleblower case lingered in court, I continued working for Gary Davis. His title by then was County Mayor. The Tennessee General Assembly had made the change. A complex series of events unfolded during that period that strained and broke my political alliance and personal relationship with Gary. The cleaving of our relationship was disappointing. Common interests had forged a relationship I'd believed would endure. It ended because momentary expediency became more important to Gary than my loyalty.

During the Jim Whitlock trial, Gary had to testify against his will. Gary saw his involvement in the court case as a political negative. His testimony obliged him to be more open about his role. It showed Gary to be more knowledgeable and more culpable than he wished to admit. He worried hospital supporters would field a candidate against him in his 2006 reelection campaign. Gary resented me for having put his campaign at risk with my actions.

Gary was also unhappy I had filed the lawsuit against Bradley Memorial Hospital to begin with. Every time the case appeared in the news, he got calls from the hospital and Jim Whitlock supporters. They asked how his executive assistant, a county employee, could sue another county institution. Gary's displeasure was apparent even though he had hired me with full knowledge that I might file a civil case. More than once, displaying his annoyance, Gary said that various people had pressured him to fire me because of it.

My response was, "Well, Gary, I was upfront. You knew a lawsuit was possible."

The situation reached a new level of stress in March 2005, when the Bradley Memorial Hospital Board of Trustees invited five hospital management companies to make proposals to buy the hospital.

In the years following my departure from the hospital, I had warned Gary that such an event was coming. I told him he should not get too close to Bradley Memorial's new board members and management.

"Gary, there will come a day when hospital officials will come to your office and let you know they can't make payroll for the month. Prepare yourself for that."

And that is what happened precisely. By then, Alan Watson had become the hospital's administrator, and Herbert Lackey was its chairman of the board. They informed Gary that Bradley Memorial would not be able to make its payroll and needed help. They requested the county extend a line of credit until the hospital could be sold.

What I told Gary was not just an opinion. Facts from the hospital's audited financial statements over the past few years backed me up. Auditors reported that there was "substantial doubt about Bradley Memorial Hospital's ability to continue as a going concern." For auditors, "doubt" refers specifically to circumstances wherein they detect an entity may be unable to meet its obligations. "Substantial doubt" predicts that such a calamity could occur within one year after the financial statement's issuance. In accounting, the "going concern" principle assumes that an entity will remain in business for the near future. Conversely, it means that the organization will not have to halt operations nor liquidate its assets in the near term at what may be low fire-sale prices.

Gary ignored my advice, appearing in a newspaper photo looking over favorable financial reports with the hospital's CFO.

By June, Community Health Systems responded to the hospital's request for proposals. They unveiled a $76.5-million offer to buy the assets of Bradley Memorial Hospital. The bid also included a pledge to invest thirty-five to forty million dollars over the next five years to bring in new services and new construction. Under the plan, Cleveland Community Hospital and Bradley Memorial would merge. Bradley Memorial would focus on emergency and inpatient medical services, while Cleveland Community would handle imaging and behavioral health services. CHS promised no one would lose their job through the consolidation. Rumors also circulated that even the senior management of Bradley Memorial had been promised jobs in exchange for their support. Erlanger Health Systems and Nashville-based Hospital Corporation of America also wrote letters of interest but sent no proposals.

Since the end of the Jim Whitlock era, only positive stories had come from Bradley Memorial. Board chairman Herbert Lackey and Alan Watson promoted the reports. Alan had been named the administrator after the forced resignation of John Barnes. As chairman of the board, Herbert had orchestrated the ouster to appoint his family friend to the job. I knew Alan Watson and had appointed him the director of imaging services during my years at Bradley Memorial. Alan was a competent clinical director, but I knew he was in over his head in his new role as the administrator.

The proposed sale shocked much of the community. Hospital claims made at county commission meetings detailing their accomplishments bolstered the view of a successful hospital. It was all a ruse. Gary believed these rosy assessments over my dire prediction.

CHS's proposal would give Bradley Memorial all of the $76.5-million payment. It required them to pay off their existing debts from this sum. That arrangement meant that some of the money would end up paying for whatever amount I would get from a settlement or verdict in my whistleblower lawsuit. This predicament became another contentious issue with my detractors and with Gary.

The sale became a certainty, as Gary and the county commission were unwilling to invest the needed funds to save Bradley Memorial Hospital as a county asset. After the parties finalized the deal, neither Alan Watson nor any other senior manager retained their jobs.

The county commission and the hospital Board of Trustees formed a joint committee to work out the details. The main contention was over who was to control the net proceeds estimated at thirty million dollars. The Board of Trustees wanted to stay in business after the hospital's wind-down period to distribute the funds. In contrast, the county commission wanted to control them. After the sale on October 1, 2005, the hospital trustees sued the county for control. It was an unpopular decision that created hostility between county commissioners and board members.

Gary was in the middle. He helped negotiate a compromise wherein the Board of Trustees dropped their suit and agreed to split the money. Bradley County got half. A special allocation panel set up within the United Way of Bradley County got the other half. Each group's mission was to distribute funding only for healthcare, wellness, or quality of life initiatives.

Each of these funds was to be perpetual. There was a prohibition of spending the principal. Reinvestment of a minimum of fifteen percent of all interest earned would go back into the principal so that the time value of money would not erode the fund over time.

The county commission later set up the Healthy Community Initiative of Bradley County to recommend allocations for their approval.

Although there was no formal agreement to do so, the United Way concentrated on new and innovative programs, while the county emphasized capital projects.

Within this environment, my lawsuit against Bradley Memorial once again took center stage within the community. As chairman of the hospital's Board of Trustees, my old adversary, Herbert Lackey, led the dialogue. Herbert was now able to exact reprisal on me for all his grievances of the past, and he did all he could do to do just that. He denounced my lawsuit against the hospital at every opportunity, saying it was unseemly for me to be suing the hospital and still working for the county.

Herbert became an obstacle to moving my lawsuit forward. He fought it at every turn and refused to authorize even a nominal settlement. When finally pressed to move forward, Herbert sent the hospital's CFO to mediation, a negotiation meeting to work out an agreement. The session did not last long, as he admitted the hospital would offer a maximum of only ten thousand dollars to settle the matter. The hospital board would not agree to a higher amount. It was an increase from the hospital's original offer of two thousand dollars. The meeting was a tremendous waste of time and resources.

Herbert also pointed to the payout all vested employees had received from the hospital's defined benefit pension plan. With the buyout, it was ending. He told me I would get a six-figure sum, and I should be happy with that. This information circulated throughout the various political circles.

Others echoed Herbert Lackey's opinion about my lawsuit. They pressured Gary to do something about his executive assistant. I stood to gain thousands at the expense of the community. Better use of the money would have been on healthcare, wellness, and quality of life.

CHAPTER
19

There were other issues between 2004 and 2005. On committees and in dealing with the county commission, Gary and I often played Good Cop versus Bad Cop, where Gary played the sympathizer and I played the aggressor. For instance, Gary knew specific regulations were unpopular but mandated. He would express his opposition at county commission meetings. At the same time, my job was to get the rule adopted. Gary drew compliments for his disapproval while I garnered complaints.

Gary's response to grumblers would go something like this: "I'll talk to Michael, but sometimes he has ideas of his own."

I mistakenly had full faith Gary would continue to back me after each game was played out. We used this approach in the adoption of stormwater regulations. Bradley County's population had hit a threshold that placed it under the Clean Water Act's authority. This law mandated rules for the entire county to manage stormwater issues in all waterways. It was a radical idea in a county that kept an agrarian outlook even as it had become increasingly urban.

The county commission set up a task force to adopt the regulations. There were minimal standards that the county had to pass. The county commission had no recourse but to approve them or face massive fines.

I spearheaded the effort and inevitably clashed with members of the task force and the county commission. In the process, I made political enemies. The regulations passed the county commission on a narrow vote of eight to six. On the day of approval, Gary decried their passage as an unfunded mandate handed down to Bradley County from a federal bureaucracy out of control. He got applause while I got vilified.

I clashed with county commissioners who served on the fire department board over taxation for fire services, how quickly the department should expand, and where they should expand. Gary's conservative philosophy was at odds with the more liberal approach of these county commissioners. I stood for Gary's ideas, while they stood for the fire department's interests and advocated aggressive expansion. They railed against me during fire department board meetings and county commission meetings. Behind the scenes, they lobbied for my removal as Gary's executive assistant.

I was Gary's representative on the county commission's insurance committee. It was Gary's goal to push his ideas and preferences through the group using me. When it came to county employee health insurance, Gary and I employed this strategy, which was always contentious. County commissioners saw health insurance as a place to make cuts and save money. Gary did not oppose saving money, but he also did not want to perturb county employees, a critical voting bloc, by taking away benefits. As directed by Gary, I advocated for the status quo. Clashes with county commissioners became commonplace and routine. The result was an erosion of my political capital—to make me vulnerable, to set me up as a scapegoat.

As a result of conflict between the Cleveland City Council and the Bradley County Commission over each governmental entity's scope and role, Gary set up the Local Government Study Committee. He commissioned community leaders to look at various government areas to see where consolidation might help the community. They reviewed issues both large and small. Officially, Gary was neutral, but behind the scenes, he asked me to probe and serve as an advocate on specific ideas as a member of the task force. The group proposed the consolidation of law enforcement and merging the city and county fire departments. They also considered a complete merger of the city and county governments. The committee's recommendations went nowhere. I took the criticism from both city and county elected officials opposed to any kind of consolidation, those who stood to lose from a merger of services.

In a reversal of this Good Cop versus Bad Cop strategy, Gary assigned me to individual county commissioners he found challenging to work with or could not abide. My job was to develop relationships with them, get to know what they were thinking, and try to bring them along on Gary's proposals.

While Gary assigned other county commissioners to me, it was Lisa Stanbery he liked least. Unlike Gary, I found Lisa to be a person with whom I could work. We developed a good rapport. I helped Lisa with many of her favorite ideas, always reporting to Gary what she was doing. Over time, my link with Lisa became problematic from Gary's perspective. He believed I was the strategist behind the many proposals she brought to the county commission, many of which Gary opposed.

Gary's suspicions were unfounded in that my loyalty was always with him. It did not matter that I gave him advance notice of what Lisa was doing. Gary could not get past this mistrust. It became extreme after Lisa's reelection to the county commission in 2006, when she announced she was considering a run against Gary for county mayor in 2010.

Over time, the Good Cop versus Bad Cop strategy took a political toll on me. It also created political trouble for Gary since those I upset pressured him about my continued county employment. Even though I was doing his bidding, Gary began blaming me for the predicament.

❖ ❖ ❖

Republican party politics and the 2006 elections also played a crucial role in my schism with Gary. From the beginning of my service with him, Gary insisted I stay involved with the local party. Gary wanted me to be his eyes, ears, and advocate within the party, to help deter any political opposition he might meet. This role brought me into conflict with other elected officials, candidates, and their supporters from time to time.

In March 2005, the Bradley County Republican Party elected Steve Crump chairman. It was a stepping-stone for him in that he intended to use it to launch a political career. During the previous eight years, which I had spent as chairman and then as a former chairman, the Republican party bylaws had given me a voting position on the executive committee, the most powerful body within the local party. But my term was finally ending. To continue as a member of the executive committee, I agreed to serve as treasurer, an essential role, but one less visible than chairman. As members of the executive committee, Steve and I began working closely together. We could not have envisioned how badly things would turn out.

One of the prominent roles of any party official is to support incumbents and discourage primary opponents. This job was difficult, given that Bradley County was supermajority Republican. Those interested in running for office within the county had to do one of two things. They either had to wait for an officeholder to retire or challenge an incumbent in the primary. Primary elections were almost equivalent to winning the general election that followed. If an incumbent had a primary opponent, executive committee members, according to the bylaws, had to remain officially neutral and supply the same resources to each candidate. Executive committee members had their personal preferences—usually the incumbent—but regardless, they had to be publicly impartial. Over the years, this bylaw provision had worked well, even when candidates accused members of being partial. Tim Gobble, who announced he was challenging the long-time incumbent sheriff in the 2006 Republican primary, took such accusations to a new level.

In Tennessee counties, the two most powerful officeholders are the county mayor and the sheriff. Their authority comes from their duties as spelled out in the Tennessee Constitution. There are many other county officials, all elected by the voters. Still, Gary, the county mayor, and Dan Gilley, the sheriff, were first among equals.

Politically, Dan had an advantage over Gary. The sheriff commanded an extensive staff and budget, which he used to his advantage. Who wanted to challenge someone who could control such a significant voting bloc? Besides employees, there were family and friends to consider.

On the other hand, Gary had an advantage over Dan in that, as the county mayor, he controlled the budget process. This dynamic resulted in clashes and mistrust between the two. The county mayor drew up and sent a proposed budget to the county commission each year for approval. All departmental forecasts, including the sheriff's, had to go through Gary, which gave him a significant advantage in shaping the outcome.

All elected officials resented this budget process. By necessity, they either had to curry favor with Gary to get what they wanted or risk his disapproval by taking their budget requests directly to the county commission. Dan Gilley was particularly at odds with this approach. He often appealed to the county commission to get what he wanted.

Gary sometimes took the budgeting process to extremes. A good example involved the circuit court clerk, who requested more funding to hire extra staff.

The clerk argued that an increased workload justified an increase.

Gary rejected her appeal, as did the county commission. Not willing to give up, the circuit court clerk filed a lawsuit in Chancery Court. After hearing arguments, one in which Gary enthusiastically testified, the chancellor offered a split decision, awarding the clerk added help but not the entire amount requested.

Before the case went to court, I told Gary he should not testify because it could lead to him attracting an opponent from among the circuit court clerk supporters.

"I'll do my duty any time someone files a lawsuit against the county, even if it means I get defeated," Gary insisted.

"Gary, there are other ways to handle this," I protested. "Do you want to draw an opponent over a budget fight? You should not be fighting other elected officeholders. The county commission denied her the money; let the county commission chairman go to court. It's not your responsibility. I know you'll do what you feel you need to do, but there will be consequences."

And that's just what Gary did, and it was just what Gary got. The circuit court clerk's son announced plans to seek the Republican Party nomination for county mayor in 2006.

❖ ❖ ❖

In Tim Gobble's challenge to Sheriff Dan Gilley in the Republican primary, Gary saw the potential for both a political ally and a sheriff with whom he could have a good relationship. Tim and Gary were friends who attended the same church. Because they had known each other for years, Gary supported Tim's candidacy. I was suspicious. I had never trusted Tim Gobble from the time I first met him. I believed him to be dishonest and secretive. There was something behind his friendly, outgoing persona I found to be fake. I thought he was manipulative. I did not trust Tim Gobble.

Additionally, he was the nephew of Juanita Burris, Jim Whitlock's administrative assistant. I had embarrassed Juanita in Jim's criminal case by revealing that she had used her position at the hospital to help Jim's floral business. I had upset her family. In my view, Tim probably hated me for it.

It was these diametrically opposing views of Tim Gobble that finally ended my relationship with Gary Davis.

Tim had previously considered running for sheriff in 1998. As a special agent for the United States Secret Service, he had impeccable credentials for the job.

When he asked me about the possibility, I was cordial but discouraged Tim from challenging the incumbent sheriff. "I'll acknowledge that Dan Gilley has created political problems for himself. Over the years, he has lost contact with the voters, unnecessarily created division within his department, and is often unapproachable. But the sheriff's office is scandal-free. I do not believe these failures call for an opponent. I'll support Dan for reelection."

When I told Tim this, I saw a brief flash of anger, followed by a broad smile. After getting similar responses from other opinion leaders, Tim did not run for sheriff in 1998. It was that brief twinkle of fury in Tim's eyes that led to my first distrust.

Later, Tim transferred from Washington, D.C., to the Chattanooga Secret Service office and used his homecoming to launch a political career in Cleveland as a city council member. Tim was able to run for this office and continue working for the Secret Service because the city council position was a nonpartisan office.

Tim immediately began targeting Cleveland's police chief, alleging abuse of office. He latched onto issues raised by a group of police officers under the chief's command. They wrote, signed, and sent to the district attorney general's office a memorandum accusing the chief of official misconduct. They cited numerous instances. The controversy swirled for months. Finally, after an extensive investigation, Jerry Estes announced no grounds for the accusations.

The broader law enforcement community resented Tim's role in the local dispute because they believed he had disrespected them all by going after the chief so aggressively. Tim resigned from the city council. After that, his supervisor transferred him back to Washington, D.C. Tim quit his job rather than return.

To make a living, Tim began consulting in the areas of law enforcement and safety. In December 2004, Gary Davis offered Tim a political lifeline by appointing him Director of the Cleveland/Bradley County Emergency Management Agency. Tim then used this position to launch his bid for sheriff in 2006.

CHAPTER
20

As 2006 began, I faced huge political and personal problems. I had actively pursued the idea of running for circuit court clerk in the May 2, 2006, Republican primary. The office was open because the incumbent had decided not to seek reelection. The idea of an elected office appealed to me to transition from working as Gary Davis's executive assistant. Gary saw me more as a liability than an asset. My job was ending. Getting elected circuit court clerk would be an effective way out for both of us. I set up a campaign structure and began making preliminary plans.

However, the many years of fighting Bradley Memorial had taken a personal toll. My wife had become increasingly unhappy. Financial worries and anxiety caused by a perceived loss of stature in the community had negatively impacted our relationship. Over the previous several years, my wife had grown discontent to the point that divorce was her only answer. It was something I had not anticipated or wanted. I dealt with the situation as privately as I could until it finally broke out publicly.

Pursuing elective office also proved difficult as the circuit court clerk soon endorsed her senior clerk's bid. It was an unexpected occurrence, making an outsider's path to victory difficult. Coupled with my impending divorce, I determined that running for that office would not be a viable option at that time.

It was a long ballot election year in 2006, which occurred once every eight years in Tennessee. It happened when all the judges who hold eight-year terms—state, district, and county; district attorneys general; and district public defenders—stand for election. They appear alongside all the other two- and four-year term officeholders.

With the announcement by Jerry Estes that he would not seek re-election for Tenth District Attorney General, Steve Crump quickly announced he was running for office. The counties of Bradley, McMinn, Monroe, and Polk compose the tenth district region. Bradley was the largest county in the tenth district. The area, unlike Bradley County, was more balanced between Republicans and Democrats. Overall, the district still favored Republicans, but a Democrat could complete. Because of this factor, two well-known Democrats jumped into the primary. Jimmy Logan, my attorney and political advisor, would face retiring criminal court judge Steve Bebb in the Democratic primary. One of them would face Steve Crump, who had only nominal opposition in the Republican primary.

Gary faced a Republican primary challenge caused by his own actions, while Sheriff Gilley faced Tim Gobble for the Republican nomination. In Bradley County, the sheriff's race by far overshadowed all the others. It was wild and nasty.

I worked in Gary's campaign, as I had done in 2002, serving as treasurer, fundraiser, and coordinator of rallies and events. I worked in this role while continuing to serve on the Republican Party Executive Committee. I exempted myself from the requirement of neutrality in a contested primary race as I had done in 2002 because it was part of my job. I had no choice.

I warned Gary he should stay out of the sheriff's race and concentrate on his own. I told Gary that his opponent was a troubling challenger, and he should focus his efforts exclusively on him. Publicly, Gary stayed neutral, but behind the scenes, he fully supported Tim's campaign, offered advice, and passed along valuable information. Tim ran a scorched earth campaign in which he assumed that anyone not enthusiastically for him was an enemy. Tim came to my office, asking for my support. I told him I would stay neutral, citing my work in Gary's campaign and my role with the party's executive committee as the reasons. After he left, I knew if Tim Gobble became sheriff, I would be in political trouble with his faction.

In February 2006, the twenty-fourth district state representative office opened unexpectedly. The incumbent announced he was running instead for the ninth district state senate seat. Again, because of my growing unease working for Gary, I decided to take a second look at running for political office as a workable way out. By then, the legal issues surrounding my impending divorce had settled down. Because all the Bradley County judges had recused themselves, just as they had done in my whistleblower case, the proceedings had been moved to Roan County, an hour and a half drive north of Cleveland. I was confident the proceedings there would avoid publicity and not be an issue.

The state primary race was not until August 3, long after the May 2 local primary. If Tim Gobble lost the race for sheriff, I had a decent chance at election. The filing deadline for the state representative seat was in April. It meant I would have to declare for the August state primary election before knowing the May county's outcome.

After announcing myself as a candidate, I quickly became a political target. An old nemesis, Jim Sharp, attacked me. I had almost run against him for county executive in 1990. Jim ended up losing to Donna Hubbard that year but had always resented me for daring to challenge him. Both of us were at a party function when Jim dressed me down for running against his preferred state representative candidate. "You are not in a position to run for political office. You have too much baggage. Your choice of lawyers is a big liability. Why would you choose Jimmy Logan, the biggest Democrat in Bradley County, to represent you in a divorce while he's running for district attorney general?"

It was true. I had employed Jimmy to represent me.

"I retained Jimmy Logan for an issue that has nothing to do with us running for political office," I responded. "I prefer to have the best lawyer I can get."

Jim Sharp was not the only one upset about my association with Jimmy Logan. Steve Crump also expressed his disapproval. Jimmy could be his opponent in the general election.

Tim Gobble and his campaign also weighed in, casting doubt on my Republican credentials to undermine my campaign. They also falsely accused me of distributing a letter from the United States Office of Special Counsel (OSC).

The OSC held that Tim Gobble had violated the Hatch Act by seeking a partisan political office. The act prohibited him from running for such an office while also serving as Director of the Cleveland/Bradley County Emergency Management Agency. The federal Hatch Act covered him since, as the director, he oversaw federal funds distribution.

Gary had kept the letter secret, only producing it after the local press began making inquiries. Gary gave me a copy of the Hatch Act letter that the Gobble campaign accused me of circulating only after its public disclosure. As a result, Tim resigned as director in April 2006, a month before the sheriff's primary election.

"Gary, you should have taken action on this letter when you first got it," I chided. "You were not honest with the public."

Gary became extremely angry with me. He likely knew that I was right but preferred not to acknowledge his deception.

Tim Gobble and his supporters also attacked the Bradley County

Republican Party Executive Committee, on which I sat. They accused the committee of bias, of supporting Dan Gilley's reelection over his own. Tim's supporters showed up at the monthly meetings to intimidate members who had loyally served the party for years. They attacked Steve Crump and me for continuing to work on the executive committee while running for office, even though each of us had stepped aside temporarily while we ran our campaigns. The party's vice-chairman served as acting chairman; the party's vice-treasurer served as acting treasurer. Both of us held onto our seats rather than resign to prevent Tim Gobble's group from potentially winning two seats on the executive committee.

Tim pressed ahead with his attacks on Sheriff Gilley. He took advantage of all Dan's vulnerabilities and accused him of being out of touch with the voters. Tim promised that, if chosen, he would be a more responsive sheriff, listen to the public, and hold open meetings for them to discuss their concerns.

Dan Gilley was a weary, exhausted candidate. He had no answers to Tim's attacks. Many of his deputies, tired of the divisions within the department, deserted him.

Tim Gobble won the primary with an unprecedented eighty-five percent of the vote, a resounding victory. Tim's margin bulged because of Democrats who crossed over to vote for him in the Republican primary. In Tennessee, voters do not register by party. They may choose each year the primary election in which they wish to participate.

Gary won comfortably against his opponent for county mayor. Steve Crump won easily to become the Republican nominee for district attorney general.

In the Democratic primary, in what many believed was an election upset, the retiring criminal court judge, Steve Bebb, beat Jimmy Logan by a small margin to garner that nomination. Jimmy's defeat was attributable to Democrats crossing over to vote for Tim Gobble in the

Republican primary. These lost votes could have helped Jimmy overcome Steve Bebb's districtwide total.

Steve Crump was disappointed, believing that the easier opponent for him was Jimmy Logan. Steve Bebb was popular in the outlying counties, while Jimmy was more of an unknown there. Conversely, Jimmy Logan was extremely unpopular among Republicans in Bradley County, while Steve Bebb had much more respect. Because of these factors, the August general election had gotten more problematic for Steve Crump.

❖ ❖ ❖

In the weeks following the May 2, 2006, primary, Tim Gobble became overly aggressive in taking on his political enemies, both perceived and real. He was able to fight them because he had only token opposition in the August general election.

His supporters showed up at the May Republican meeting and tried to take over the party. After finding out the executive committee functioned under bylaws prescribed by the state party, they backed off.

Two of Tim's closest strategists and most vocal supporters came to my office and got a copy of the bylaws. The rules were too much for Tim's supporters to overcome because they made it difficult for an outside group to take over the party apparatus. His supporters were extremely disappointed.

As Tim Gobble's group continued to attack the executive committee, Steve Crump suddenly resigned as chairman. The acting chairman, influenced by the growing Gobble faction, then publicly demanded my resignation. Unlike Steve, who did not want party politics to ruin his chance at election, I refused. After Tim Gobble's win, I had concluded my campaign was already a lost cause. I would stay on the executive committee and help prevent its takeover by Tim's side.

The following month, the executive committee installed a new chairman and vice-chairman. The acting chairman had resigned after failing to get me to leave. Members of the committee believed the new chairman could bridge the chasm between the party and Tim's group. He had a good reputation in both camps.

However, his leadership did not keep the Gobble faction from setting up a counter organization. It was a rump party with no authority. Its function was to serve as a support source for Tim Gobble and criticize the regular party and its officials.

The executive committee got more criticism after reluctantly voting to call for the resignation of the twenty-second district state representative. Authorities had arrested him in Nashville for taking bribes. The representative's area covered much of rural Bradley County, and he had been resisting growing calls for him to quit. While it was clear to the committee that we'd had no choice but to ask him to resign, some in the party felt we had betrayed the representative, that he was innocent until proven guilty. We were more focused on keeping the seat.

Our action was decisive. The representative sent in his letter of resignation. The Gobble group was quick to cast ridicule on the executive committee for taking this public action.

I talked to Gary about the twenty-fourth state representative race. Since I had concluded I could not win, I wanted to withdraw.

Gary would not hear of it. "Michael, you have no choice. I'm getting pressure from all sides. They all want me to fire you. Stay in the race; make a good showing. I'll make adjustments later."

I did as he instructed. I took a leave of absence from my job in July to raise money and campaign. Fundraising was difficult, but I did amass some funds. Still, it took ten thousand additional dollars out of my pocket to make a decent showing.

As expected, I faced significant opposition from Tim Gobble's supporters. The most effective tool used was an online forum called

Hometown Cleveland. Set up by Gobble supporters, it had success-fully taken down Sheriff Gilley in the May primary. The forum now turned its attention to the August elections. Not only was I vilified, but so too was Steve Crump and anyone else who was Tim's enemy. The attacks became so vile and outrageous that I finally quit reading the criticisms.

I warned Gary, "If you fire me, I will be the first person in Brad-ley County to lose their job because of an online political forum. You shouldn't be reading that nonsense. Those comments represent an ex-treme minority view."

Gary was unimpressed by my argument.

Steve Crump did not fare any better against Tim Gobble. In a gesture to his Democratic supporters who crossed over to vote for him in the Republican primary, Tim supported and actively worked for the election of Democrat Steve Bebb for district attorney general. It was also payback for Steve Crump's role as party chairman.

The result of Tim Gobble's opposition was that I lost. But because of the money I contributed to my campaign, I made a decent showing. Gary congratulated me on a well-run race.

Steve Crump lost narrowly to Steve Bebb. Tim Gobble proved to be the big winner. He quickly rolled through both the May and August elections.

CHAPTER
21

After August 3, 2006, I returned to my old job as executive assistant to Gary Davis, knowing that my time there was probably ending. Too much had happened. Bad relations with Gary, county commissioners, and others had taken their toll. Running for elective office, Tim Gobble's opposition, and other such things were also factors.

Attacks from hospital board members, led by board chairman Herbert Lackey, leading up to my whistleblower lawsuit's settlement had gotten the attention of my opponents. They had spread the rumor everywhere I was getting one million dollars in compensation.

I did not know when or how, but I expected Gary would fire me. But I knew him well enough to know it would not happen right away. He would wait until things had settled down. I planned to use the time to find a new job.

On September 1, 2006, all the newly elected officials took their oaths of office. It was a big event, held outside in front of the Bradley County Courthouse. Gary must have felt a new day was dawning in the county government. He now had a sheriff he could work with, an ally. Being friends and attending church together meant they could share power. Life was good for him.

An event occurred the day before the swearing-in that reinforced Gary's belief that I was a liability. He received a letter of complaint about the sheriff's office from the Tennessee Occupational Safety and Health Administration (TOSHA). It entailed issues from Dan Gilley's administration, but the new sheriff would have to deal with them. As the county's risk manager, it was my responsibility to investigate and report back to TOSHA with a resolution.

When I saw the complaint, I knew it meant trouble. Gary knew it too, but he sent me to investigate anyway.

I met with Sheriff Gobble and his administrative staff. We toured the facility. Afterward, I sought advice on how to resolve the issue. After writing a plan, I would have Gobble's staff review it. I promised to keep them apprised, to send them copies of all correspondence between TOSHA and me. But by the time I got back to Gary's office, the sheriff's office had inundated him with calls wanting to know what my motive was for starting the complaint.

Gary told me, "This is the kind of thing I'm going to be dealing with from here on out."

❖ ❖ ❖

It took only a few weeks for Gary's relationship with Tim Gobble to sour. Right after the swearing-in, I had irritated Gary about the likelihood of this happening. "You know, it will not be long before Tim turns on you. He will demand more money for the sheriff's budget, and what will you do then?"

Gary had been dismissive of my comments, believing them to be bitter words, but they proved prophetic. It was a shock to Gary when Tim began to oppose the old rules and cause trouble. After reviewing his budget, Tim came before the Bradley County Commission demanding more money. He made the case that his accounts were woefully deficient. Tim wanted added funding, and he did not want to wait until next year's budget cycle to get it. Tim's request infuriated Gary and most county commissioners too. They denied his request. The sparring continued for several weeks.

Tim would not take no for an answer. He filed a lawsuit in Chancery Court seeking the funds anyway. Gary testified in opposition. Tim lost the case. Gary's grand alliance with the sheriff ended before it began.

After the lawsuit, Gary sheepishly said to me, "Go ahead and tell me, 'I told you so.'"

"No, Gary," I responded. "There is no need. You already said it."

CHAPTER
22

Seven years after Jim Whitlock called me to his office at Bradley Memorial Hospital, I settled my whistleblower lawsuit. On September 27, 1999, the ordeal began when Jim offered me six months' severance pay if I left quietly. It ended on September 13, 2006, the day I accepted an agreement with the hospital board. It was not a difficult decision.

By September 2006, the value of my lawsuit had diminished due to the sale of the hospital. Even though I still had a good case, going to trial against Bradley Memorial Hospital would have been challenging in wind-down status. I was uncertain a jury would see the merits of prosecuting such an old case of retaliation with an entity that no longer existed.

When the hospital sold, one million dollars had been set aside in the budget to resolve several lawsuits. My whistleblower case was just one of them. It was this one-million-dollar figure that my opponents had circulated as the amount I would be getting.

As 2006 progressed, Harry Burnette, my attorney, had become concerned that we needed to speed the case along. Now, with the primary over, he began pushing the hospital's attorneys to make a serious settlement offer, or we would set a trial date. Finally, the hospital attorneys were able to engage Herbert Lackey and the other hospital board members in a meaningful discussion of a court trial's merits versus a settlement. As a result, they offered me one hundred thousand dollars to settle. It was a split decision, as some of the board members objected. They believed the settlement offer was too high.

With Harry's assurance that the settlement offer was the best he could do, I accepted it. I received the check on October 5, 2006, and signed the release. Because Harry took the case on consignment, I received sixty percent, or sixty thousand dollars; he received forty percent, or forty thousand dollars. I convinced him to pay the expenses of twenty-three hundred dollars from his part of the proceeds and not mine. It was a request because our contract said I paid for all costs. I told Harry that sixty thousand dollars was a small amount for all I had experienced. He agreed. I realized my share was about the same amount I would have received back in 1999 if I had accepted Jim Whitlock's severance offer.

On October 9, 2006, I told Gary about the settlement and the amount. I do not think he believed me. He had heard the million-dollar rumor for months.

Since there was no nondisclosure agreement, I prepared a press release about the settlement. It pointed out the deal did not include deniability on the part of Bradley Memorial, which was a huge concession. I chose not to issue my official statement until the hospital released an announcement. I wanted to avoid publicity if possible, because I was still trying to save my job with Gary. Amazingly, Herbert Lackey and the hospital board did not release one either. I imagined they were trying to keep the settlement quiet also, to avoid the criticism they would get for settling.

My silence on the settlement did not save me with Gary. Even though I had expected some move by him, I was surprised when it happened. On October 18, 2006, Gary called me to his office. He told me I would report at once to the Cleveland/Bradley County Emergency Management Agency as their new administrative officer. I would oversee office matters.

"Gary, you know I have no background in emergency management," I objected. "Those men over there will be suspicious and resent me being there."

"It's the only place I've been able to find. It's that job or nothing."

Gary's stark assessment made me realize if I were going to continue working, I had to accept the assignment. Not wanting to be unemployed, I took the job, rationalizing that I could use the time to look for other work.

Gary also informed me, "Your salary will be cut by one thousand dollars annually. That's the best I can do with their budget constraints." I thought that was ironic given how overfunded the agency was.

The organization had a history of bad management. Gary had fired the EMA director before naming Tim Gobble to the post. The move was necessary, as the former director faced charges of official misconduct.

There were too many people at the EMA and not enough work. I envisioned having to sit around with men who did not want me there. They would be suspicious. I knew there would be an adverse outcome.

After Tim Gobble's forced resignation from the EMA, Gary had appointed a new director, one of the least qualified individuals who applied. The new director was more of a foot soldier than a director, but Gary preferred him. He was compliant, would not cause trouble, and would have no higher ambition. Gary sent me there to aid him with writing and updating emergency plans, something the new director would have a tough time doing without help.

I got a chilly reception. The EMA staff shunned me, and the tension was palpable. One of them told me I had "brought politics into the department." I hated being there. My stay was short.

From my observation, the biggest decision made in the office each day was where and with which other emergency responders the three staff members would meet for lunch. They got excited when police, fire, or paramedics left on calls. Even though they had no reason to go, each person jumped into his county vehicle and sped off to the site anyway. They spent a lot of time washing their emergency vehicles.

Tim Gobble came around, often looking suspiciously at me, always with a slightly scornful smile.

I endured until May 11, 2007, when I finally decided I'd had enough. I went to Gary to negotiate a separation agreement. I did not have another job to go to and was uncertain what I would do next. I wanted an official deal that would protect me from any county employee who might entertain the idea of disparaging me after my departure. I was sure that would happen without a contract preventing it. Gary agreed to the separation agreement, including a non-disparagement requirement, ending my seven years of employment with Bradley County.

EPILOGUE

I never worked in healthcare or government again. I stayed in Cleveland, Tennessee, for a few years after leaving my job with Bradley County. Later, I returned home to my native western North Carolina. After more than thirty years, I left the place where I had spent my entire career. I moved to Asheville, North Carolina, and have lived in relative obscurity for a decade. I jokingly told Jimmy Logan when I left that I was going into exile, but it has not been that way at all. I still have family and friends in Cleveland, and I feel free to go back to visit anytime I want.

I've had more than twenty years to reflect on my experience of 1999 and the years following. I am not bitter; I am not a victim. I am not a hero, and I am also not a villain. Given the circumstances and dynamics surrounding those events, the decisions I made were the only options I felt I had. From my perspective, I couldn't have escaped them any more than water can avoid running downhill. Deep inside, something told me to rise to the challenge, face the issues, and fight to the finish. I would have been deeply disappointed in myself if I hadn't. My decision does not haunt me. I have no regrets. I am saddened, though—saddened that the outcome wasn't the resounding victory for which I'd so dearly fought.

ABOUT THE AUTHOR

Michael K. Willis was born and raised in the Appalachian region of the Blue Ridge Mountains in western North Carolina. He received his bachelor's degree in political science and history from Western Carolina University and his master's degree in public administration from the University of Tennessee at Knoxville. After college, Willis moved to Cleveland, Tennessee, where he spent the next three decades working in county government, most notably as the assistant administrator at Bradley Memorial Hospital. In 2010, Willis returned to his native home. He currently lives in Asheville, North Carolina. Willis is also the author of *The Life of Mikey: A Memoir.*

* 9 7 8 1 9 5 3 0 2 1 5 7 1 *